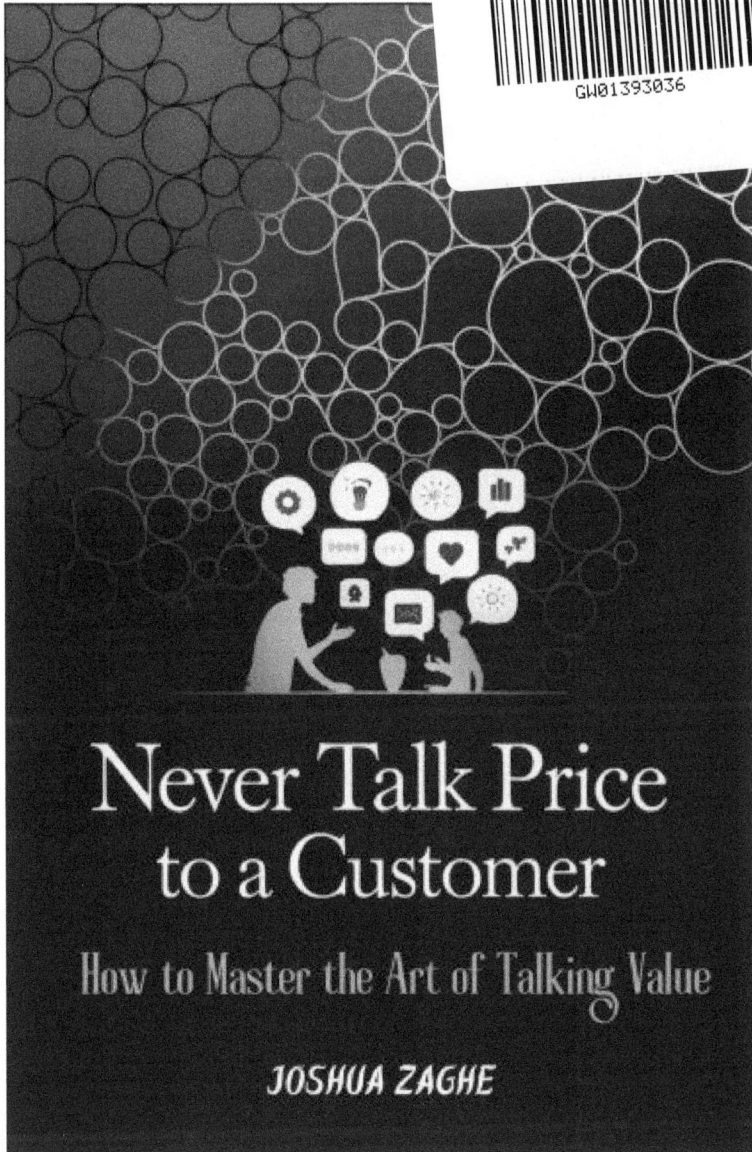

Never Talk Price to a Customer

How to Master the Art of Talking Value

JOSHUA ZAGHE

Never Talk Price to a Customer: How to Master the Art of Talking Value

JOSHUA ZAGHE

Published by BILLY GRANT, 2024.

NEVER TALK PRICE TO A CUSTOMER: HOW TO MASTER THE ART OF TALKING VALUE

First edition. October 5, 2024.

Copyright © 2024 JOSHUA ZAGHE.

ISBN: 979-8227621962

Written by JOSHUA ZAGHE.

Also by JOSHUA ZAGHE

Table of Contents

*To my mentor **Vusi Thembekwayo**.*

INTRODUCTION

IN A WORLD WHERE STATISTICS and numbers seem to set the parameters for interaction, it is simple to talk about prices with clients. What if I told you that the most prosperous businesspeople worldwide are multilingual? A language with depth, sensibility, and emotional resonance that goes beyond simple numerical representations.

Introducing "Never Talk Price to a Customer: How to Master the Art of Talking Value," a game-changing book.

Imagine this: Someone asks you what you do for a living at a dinner party. You hesitate, ready yourself for the inevitable follow-up question—"How much do you charge?It's practically as foreseeable as the Christmas season when someone pulls out the notorious fruitcake. But what if you told a compelling tale about the impact of your job in place of providing a price?

❧

NOT WITH YOUR PRICE, but with the sheer worth of what you have to offer, you could light up the room. You may infuse your business narrative with energy and turn the conversation from lifeless dollar signs to bright possibilities.

This is a tactic that sets the extraordinary apart from the mediocre, not merely wishful thinking. In the realm of entrepreneurship, there is a widespread misperception that price is everything and that your value is best expressed by your price.

❧

IN REALITY, IT'S YOUR understanding of value—the emotional connections you make, the transformation you promise—that holds the genuine power. Value-driven entrepreneurs can attract attention, engender loyalty, and forge connections that go beyond business deals.

As we go into this book, you'll learn the psychology of why value, not price, is what buyers react to. Imagine entering a dealership for high-end vehicles. Purchasing an automobile is an investment in a way of life, a brand, and a status symbol.

The salesperson's job is to portray a picture of the life you'll lead behind the wheel, not to lecture you with numbers. They discuss the svelte styling, the state-of-the-art technology, and the liberating sensation while speeding down the interstate. Suddenly, the price becomes a mere afterthought. You're investing in an experience rather than purchasing a car.

But let's face it, not everyone is inherently skilled at this art. A large number of us are accustomed to thinking in terms of expenses, savings, and competitive pricing.

If we delay starting the price discussion, we risk losing out on possible sales. The worst part is that you diminish your value as soon as you start focussing on the cost. You run the risk of being simply one more item in a sea of options, all vying for the lowest price. Nobody desires that.

We're going to debunk these misconceptions about prices because of this. We'll look at actual situations, analyse sales tactics, and uncover the potent methods used by prosperous businesspeople to shift the subject from pricing to value.

You will discover how to deflect attention from the numbers and establish yourself as the authority in your industry by doing things like framing the conversation in a novel way and crafting engrossing narratives that connect with your audience.

Consider for a second when was the last time you made a purchase. Did you go with the option that seemed right, or did you go with the cheapest one available? Which one made you excited or met a need in your life?

IT'S POSSIBLE THAT you selected that high-end brand because it offered durability, excellence, and a sense of community. This also holds true for your company. You shift the dynamic by emphasising the value your services or goods bring to the table. Instead of being just another vendor, you become a respected partner and strengthen your position.

Now picture changing your sales strategy to emphasise the advantages your clients would experience.

WHAT IF YOU STEERED the conversation towards the outcomes they can anticipate each time someone enquires about your prices? Suddenly, it's not about the money; it's about the life-enhancing possibilities. For example, you could say, "Imagine what it would feel like to save 20 hours a month with my service, freeing you up to focus on what you love most," instead of, "My service costs $500."

We'll explore the three golden rules of value discussion in this book: recognising the emotional connection, using great narrative, and establishing yourself as the authority. You will have the ability to recognise and express the distinct value that you offer, making it difficult for prospective clients to view you as anything less than indispensable.

We'll also explore common price-related mistakes encountered by entrepreneurs and how to prevent them.

⥈

WE'LL LOOK AT THE PSYCHOLOGY of consumer behaviour, the value of empathy in the sales process, and how to leave a lasting impression on potential customers so they become devoted followers. By the end, you'll have acquired useful skills and knowledge to change the way you talk to others, establishing connections based on mutual respect, trust, and indisputable value.

So fasten your seatbelt! We're going on an exciting journey through the practice of value-driven dialogue.

CHAPTER 1
THE FOUNDATION OF VALUE

Imagine entering a realm where your interactions with clients inspire genuine connection, excitement, and trust. This is about creating a foundation of value that connects intimately with your audience, not about competing on price or wrangling over numbers. That wonderful instant when attention turns from the financial signs to the extraordinary difference your good or service may make in someone's life.

Understanding that value is fluid, multidimensional, and very personal rather than a fixed number is at the core of this shift. Imagine an experienced chef cooking a dish. Every component is thoughtfully selected for the experience it provides as well as flavour. People are drawn in by the aroma that fills the air, bringing back memories and stoking cravings. You want to arouse the same sensation of eagerness in your customers when you speak with them.

Your goal is to present them with an abundance of options that will pique their interest and help them feel understood.

How therefore does one lay this foundation? Determine what makes your offering unique before anything else. What is it about your offering that really makes a difference in people's lives? Perhaps it's the way your coaching program inspires others to pursue their passions, or maybe it's the cosy, homemade touches of your crafts. It's crucial to describe that change in a way that appeals to your audience's emotions.

Consider your product or service as a key that allows your clients to enter a new realm.

An important factor in this process is empathy. Pay attention to the wants, needs, and difficulties of your clients. Every encounter is a chance to pay close attention to what they have to say and comprehend their particular situation. You start to view talks as opportunities to improve someone's life rather than just as business dealings when you approach them with this perspective. Find out by asking them questions what matters most to them.

What hurts them the most? What kind of dreams do they have? This kind of interest opens the door to deeper relationships, allowing you to craft your pitch in a way that resonates powerfully.

Spend some time compiling testimonies and anecdotes from people who have profited from your offering. The idea of value is given life by these stories. A simple testimonial has the power to change people's opinions by turning intangible benefits into real experiences. Imagine a happy customer telling you how your exercise regimen improved their lives.

Through their words, potential clients might see themselves on that journey of transformation, bridging an emotional gap.

Let's now discuss how crucial it is to centre the discussion on value as opposed to cost. It's similar to extending an invitation to a party without disclosing the cover charge. You run the risk of steering the conversation down a limited route full of uncertainties and comparisons the moment you bring up price. Rather, illustrate clearly the benefits that your clients will receive.

It's a perspective shift that places the cost as an afterthought rather than the main focus. For instance, instead of saying, "My consulting package costs $1,500," change it to, "Investing in this consulting package opens doors to a clearer business strategy, saving you countless hours of frustration and leading to a significant revenue increase."

Think about the world of upscale shopping. Ever enter a high-end retailer? It's a different environment. You're engulfed in an encounter meant to inspire sentiments of status and exclusivity.

The salespeople don't bombard you with price tags; they tell stories of craftsmanship, heritage, and the unique attributes of each piece. They captivate you with an experience that makes it easy for you to see how this product would improve your life. You have already committed yourself emotionally by the time you hear the price.

Putting this strategy into effect takes time. Play around with the words you use. Replace words that emphasise expense with ones that emphasise value and advantages.

You're providing a solution to an issue rather than just a product. This may be a life-changing shift in perspective.

Differentiating yourself from the competition is developing an emotional bond with your clients. Consider your preferred brands. They're not simply names; they conjure feelings, memories, and trust. Their audience connects strongly with the narrative their marketing methods tell. They are able to establish an emotional connection, which promotes loyalty that goes beyond business dealings.

Customers who are made to feel important by you will promote your brand to others. They become repeat customers after sharing their experiences and referring others to your services.

Authenticity is essential to keeping this relationship going. Consumers are able to detect dishonesty quite quickly. They'll be able to tell if you're not sincere in your desire to add value, and your attempts might not succeed. Talk about your personal struggles, victories, and experiences.

Show your audience who you really are—a person who is driven to positively impact their lives. Being vulnerable fosters trust, and trust is the cornerstone of any healthy partnership.

Now think about your brand and how you portray yourself. Your space's atmosphere, messaging, and even your images should reflect the value you offer. A polished website, striking logo, and interesting social media presence all speak to the calibre of your products and services.

Understanding Value vs. Price

The conflict between price and value in the sales industry sometimes seems never-ending. Value is something different from price, which is that dazzling figure that consumers see. It's the soul of that number, the pulse of what really counts. Imagine entering a bakery and being enveloped by the aroma of freshly baked goods. Though it costs $5 for the bread in front of you, what does that actually mean? Lunch breaks are made happier by more than simply bread; they're also made happier by the cosiness of a cosy morning, the warmth of a family get-together, and the beginning of a homemade sandwich. Value is far more than just price when it comes to those kinds of experiences.

Price can be expressed simply as a definite quantity devoid of any sentiment. Yet, value embodies emotion, memories, and experiences. It varies from person to person, moulded by needs, wants, and even life experiences. Imagine a mother purchasing a bicycle for her offspring. $300 for a bike may seem like an expensive price, but is it really worth it?

That's her child's smile, those carefree moments when they ride their bikes down the street, the memories made on their weekend excursions. That $300 bike means adventure, excitement, and family time to her; it's more than simply metal and rubber.

Let's dissect it a little more. Think about buying an automobile. One factor is the sticker price, but what about the excitement of the open road? The safety elements that provide peace of mind? The dependability that adds up to more family vacations and fewer repairs?

Every one of these factors matters when the consumer is making a selection. In this instance, even though a $25,000 car costs more than a less dependable model, its reliability and security may make it quite valuable.

Knowing how clients view value can change the way we interact with them. It necessitates listening intently, focussing on their narratives, and engaging with their feelings. When a customer enters a store, they are thinking about how a purchase will improve their lives rather than just the sales figures.

For them, what will it change? This perspective shift generates opportunities for connection, making every conversation significant.

As customers consider their alternatives, they often play a game of comparison, not just with other products but with their own experiences. Imagine the traveler staying at a five-star hotel. Although the hotel may cost more than a typical motel, consider the luxurious mattress, the amazing views, and the attentive staff.

⚜

THESE COMPONENTS BOOST the experience and turn a routine visit into a memorable experience. When people evaluate anything, they evaluate the experiences they can have, the issues they can resolve, and the joy they can enjoy. It turns into a puzzle where you have to match the pieces together to get a satisfying picture.

This idea of value is even more evident in the context of services. While the $150 hourly rate for a therapist may raise some eyes at first, what are your options?

When someone seeks assistance for mental health problems, they are not only seeking time but also healing, support, and direction. The benefits of therapy include enhanced relationships, personal development, and, in the end, a higher standard of living. When the potential for transformation is this great, the cost becomes insignificant.

Establishing a link between value and customer perception creates new avenues for interaction. It's critical to express the advantages precisely while avoiding the pitfalls of concentrating only on cost. When clients enquire about prices, it's an excellent chance to change the subject. Tell tales of those who have profited, rather than just offering a price. The story becomes less intimidating when the price is reframed as "Yes, the package is $1,200, but let me tell you about John, who saw his sales double within three months of our training." Value is highlighted instead of price.

Realising that every consumer has a unique perspective is essential to creating value. To someone else, what appears costly could be an absolute necessity.

Consider your preferred brand. What makes you select them? It could be their affinity for quality, their devotion to sustainability, or their capacity to fit into your way of life. That decision speaks to your sense of value, which lessens the impact of the cost.

It takes skill to navigate value-related discussions. It's about drawing clients into a story, not about making a sale. Asking questions that evoke feelings, desires, and experiences is crucial. Why did they come in today? What difficulties do they encounter?

As you pay attention, you'll find ways to present your product or service as a method to improve their lives. You turn into a journey buddy, escorting them as they learn about the advantages of what you have to offer.

Authentic connections are what customers want to see and feel. Instead of feeling like just another customer, they want to be seen and understood. Therefore, be genuine in your discussions when you discuss value. Share your passion and purpose. Tell them why you act in the ways that you do.

It's an opportunity to build a stronger relationship and trust that goes beyond a single transaction.

Think about the craft of narrative, which is an effective technique in the persuasion toolbox. Stories speak to us because they reflect our shared experiences. They arouse emotions, enticing clients to embark on a shared experience. Craft interesting narratives around your offerings, highlighting moments of transformation.

The Psychology of Pricing

Price is more than just a figure; it's a signal with psychological and emotional significance. When consumers see a price tag, a million ideas flash through their heads. This is the point at which price psychology enters the picture, tying expectations, brand loyalty, and perceived value together to create a complex web of consumer behaviour.

Imagine entering a posh store and inhaling the aroma of luxury. The expensive prices are part of their appeal, though.

Consumers are willing to pay more for a brand that represents prestige and excellence. Those heavy price tags inspire notions of exclusivity and refinement, tempting visitors to come into a world where they feel exceptional. Here, price evolves into a badge of pride, a symbol of belonging to a chosen group that enjoys the finer things in life. It's amazing how a seemingly insignificant number can arouse feelings and goals.

PRICE IMPRESSIONS ARE greatly influenced by expectations. Customers are more inclined to part with their money if they think they're obtaining something exceptional. Think about it: when a product is branded as the "best" or "premium," purchasers already approach it with a sense of anticipation. Their mindset is set up to value the experience that comes after making the purchase. Here's where marketing steps in, laying out the expectations for the consumer.

IT ALL COMES DOWN TO crafting a story that guarantees not just a worthwhile experience but also a product.

Consider the realm of technological devices. Popular brands frequently charge exorbitant rates for their new products. However, why do shoppers wait in queue outside such businesses, ready to part with their hard-earned cash? It's that psychological nudge—the conviction that possessing the newest device demonstrates creativity and state-of-the-art technology.

⁂

BASED ON THE HYPE SURROUNDING a launch and the reputation of the brand, the perceived worth soars. In this context, price becomes a talking point and a means of indicating to peers one's status and trendiness.

Another potent psychological component that shapes consumers' perceptions of pricing is brand loyalty. Customers are frequently less sensitive to price hikes when they have a sense of connection to a brand. This devotion develops gradually as a result of happy memories, emotional resonance, and trust.

Brand loyalists may have an inbuilt incentive to stick with the company, even if costs increase. When clients are willing to invest in something they believe in, the connection changes from being a simple transaction to a partnership.

Think about the devoted customer of a particular coffee brand. A dollar extra for their daily fix could be paid by that person if they identify with the brand's values of ethical business methods, sustainable sourcing, or a distinctive roasting method.

⁂

THEY BELIEVE THAT THE increased cost is a reflection of shared ideals, excellence, and honesty. Buying becomes more than just getting a coffee; it's a means to support something worthwhile. Price is perceived differently as a result of this emotional involvement, becoming a small detail in the context of a larger picture.

The notion of perceived worth is a crucial factor that influences buyers' evaluation of prices. This involves their perceptions about the product's worth in addition to what they see on the label.

A person is likely to consider the purchase of a high-quality pair of shoes to be justified if they think they will last longer and be more comfortable. After weighing the prospective long-term benefits, it becomes a logical choice.

This view is frequently connected to the idea of giving something up. Customers engage in a mental transaction when they compare the price of a product to its benefits. "Am I receiving enough value in exchange for this expense?

⟡

THE PRICE IS LESS OF a barrier if the response is more in the affirmative. For instance, an organic skincare brand may cost more, but if buyers are sold on the natural components and the outcomes they guarantee, the cost seems fair—almost like a prudent investment in self-care.

Complexity is further increased by the circumstances surrounding pricing. Imagine seeing a dress branded at $200 in a department shop, and then you learn it's 50% off during a sale. It feels like a steal now.

This circumstance alters the customer's perspective by appealing to the excitement of the transaction. That identical clothing may have been regarded costly previously, but now, its worthiness skyrockets. The way a number is presented inside a larger story is just as important to the psychology of pricing as the actual figure itself. Perceived savings, discounts, and the idea of getting a better bargain tend to influence customers.

⟡

ANOTHER PSYCHOLOGICAL phenomena that affects how people perceive prices is anchoring. Customers' minds tend to use the product's original price as a point of reference when they first see it. A smartphone that is originally priced at $999 and is then discounted to $799 seems even more appealing. That original price creates a mental anchor, making the discount feel meaningful. It's a psychological ploy to make buyers believe they've found a deal. This supports their wish to feel as though they are wise and astute about the money they spend.

Pricing perceptions can also be affected by social proof. People's attention is piqued when they witness others raving about a product, posting great reviews, or showing off their most recent purchases. Customers are more likely to buy, even if the prices seem excessive, when they receive positive feedback from their peers. Fear of missing out, or FOMO, turns into a motivating factor that pushes consumers to make purchases they might not have otherwise thought about. "I need to try this brand because everyone is talking about it!"

Gaining an understanding of your audience is necessary to create an environment that fosters these psychological variables. It's critical to understand their expectations, motives, and feelings. Consider the language used, the experiences designed around the products, and the way they are presented. Customers are far more eager to interact with pricing when they feel appreciated and understood. The goal here is to establish sincere connections that speak to each individual on a personal level, not to manipulate.

Think about using storytelling as a tool to improve self-perceptions. Customers engage with you when you tell engaging stories about your product and emphasise how it improves people's lives. They elevate the perceived value of their prospective purchase by seeing themselves as a part of that narrative. Because stories evoke strong emotions, the cost seems reasonable in exchange for a potentially life-changing experience.

CHAPTER 2
SHIFTING THE CONVERSATION

It's time to shift the focus away from numbers and towards something much more meaningful in a world where talk about numbers is all the rage. When you move the emphasis from price to the value you provide, you create an environment where connections grow and understanding blossoms. It takes more than just talking numbers to create compelling narratives that captivate readers.

Think about this: every encounter you have with a prospective client is an opportunity to tell an engaging tale. Imagine entering a busy market where vendors are fighting for customers' attention by shouting their pricing. Then, though, a voice breaks through the din, urging listeners to delve deeper than the dollar sign. This change is a concept based on authenticity, empathy, and connection rather than just a technique.

THESE DAYS, PEOPLE are more in search of experiences and answers than just goods. Consumers are curious about their gains from a transaction. People are hungry for tales of how a good or service has improved their lives. This mode of thinking, which emphasises results over expenses, transforms the way businesses communicate.

Imagine a client in search of a workout regimen. Why not illustrate the transformation with a painting instead of listing fees? Emphasise how your program helps people take back their health, gain confidence, and create a sense of community. Provide firsthand accounts from actual people who have accomplished actual results to support such assertions. Abruptly, the price tag becomes less noticeable and is eclipsed by the vivid picture of personal development.

Understanding the wants and demands of your customers is necessary for this change in communication. What do they want to accomplish? What difficulties do they encounter? When you listen well, you can use it to turn a monologue into a meaningful exchange in your conversations.

Start a conversation with your audience by posing enquiries that elicit their motives. You can customise your messaging by gathering insights from their aspirations.

Whenever you talk about value, you should emphasise the special features of what you have to offer. Consider the feelings and experiences that your audience finds compelling. Selling organic skincare products, for example, involves more than simply the components. It all boils down to the comfort that comes from knowing they're choosing things that are good for the environment and their skin. Stress the ways in which your products are consistent with their beliefs, incorporating sustainability into the story.

Perceptions are significantly shaped by visuals. Use visuals to show buyers what to expect, such as photographs and movies, rather than writing long descriptions. Show customers how the products fit into their lives in addition to what they are purchasing. Customers are more likely to understand the value of your product when they can see themselves using it.

They are able to see past the price tag thanks to this visualisation, which raises the discourse.

Using metaphors and analogies is another effective strategy. These literary techniques make links between what you're presenting and what your clients already know. If you're selling a subscription service, for example, compare it to a financial personal trainer—someone who offers direction and encouragement along the way to financial independence.

This contrast moves the emphasis from the monthly cost to the priceless advantages they will get.

In these kinds of interactions, empathy is essential. Make your customers feel heard and understood by acknowledging their worries and anxieties. Consider criticisms as doorsway to more in-depth conversations rather than writing them off as simple roadblocks. When clients show reluctance regarding cost, answer with enquiries that enable them to clarify their concerns.

THIS GIVES YOU THE opportunity to emphasise the benefits of your solution by outlining how it solves those issues.

It takes skill to move the conversation along. Redirect the discussion to outcomes when someone asks about pricing, rather than responding defensively. Don't respond defensively to a consumer who asks about an expensive item, for instance. Switch to talking about the long-term advantages instead. "I realise that this could seem like a big financial commitment.

However, many of our clients have discovered that the durability and performance greatly transcend the original cost." This approach not only answers their question but also invites them to reconsider their perspective.

Maintaining consistency throughout all touchpoints is essential to crafting an engaging story. Your social media accounts, website, and face-to-face communications should all convey the same message about value. Create a unified brand narrative that speaks to the goals of your target audience.

They will be more open to the concept of investing in your offerings when they perceive that you are consistent.

Don't be afraid to share your experience. Customers are drawn to authenticity, particularly in this day and age of increased scepticism. Tell the world about any struggles or victories your brand has had. This makes your company more approachable and enables clients to establish a personal connection with you.

PEOPLE ADORE ROOTING for the underdog; sharing your narrative can develop a bond that transcends the transactional nature of sales.

Participation from the customer enhances the discussion. Invite people to talk about their encounters using your good or service. The narrative surrounding pricing can be significantly changed with the use of user-generated material. Customers feel more justified about investing when they witness others taking advantage of what you have to offer.

Establishing a community where clients can exchange insights not only improves their experience but also establishes your company as a crucial component of their path.

In the digital age, utilising social proof becomes vital. Case studies, reviews, and testimonials help to intensify the value discussion. Prospective clients get reassured when they see the success others have attained. Distribute these tales throughout your channels so that potential customers can identify with other people's experiences.

It spreads like wildfire, bringing up topics other than just pricing.

Remain frank and honest whenever the subject of pricing comes up. Cost discussions don't have to be uncomfortable. Rather, present it as a component of the larger discussion about value. Give details about the source of goods, quality assurance, and customer service that go into your pricing. Customers are better able to recognise the actual value of the products they're considering because of this transparency, which enables them to comprehend the reasoning behind the statistics.

Remember how important it is to be flexible when the topic of discussion changes. Every client is different, having distinct requirements and tastes. Tailor your messaging to accommodate diverse audiences while retaining a constant core theme. Being adaptable enables you to address each person's unique needs and preferences, indicating your interest in their experience.

⚜

THE ULTIMATE OBJECTIVE is to cultivate a friendship based on mutual respect and understanding. Value, as opposed to price, establishes the foundation for deep connections. Customers are more likely to interact with your brand when they perceive that your demands are your first priority. The discussion turns from a straightforward exchange into a collaboration in which both sides contribute to the other's success.

The Language of Value

The way we think and communicate is shaped by language. Words have the power to either establish or destroy relationships when it comes to talks with clients. Moving away from price-centric language opens up a landscape where advantages and outcomes take center stage, allowing for a better relationship with potential purchasers. It's about sparking people's imaginations, creating a sense of possibilities, and drawing a clear image of what your service may accomplish.

Imagine hearing a steady barrage of numbers as soon as you enter a store. "This costs $100, that's on sale for $50." Instantly, the focus changes to the transaction rather than the transformation. Turn the script around and think about how various words can improve the discourse. What if you told the amazing tales of individuals who changed their lives as a result of your product, rather than concentrating on the cost? When language reflects the value rather than the cost, it cultivates excitement and engagement.

Let's look at a few strong words that arouse sentiments of worth. When you present a purchase as an investment rather than just a one-time cost, you encourage clients to perceive the long-term benefits. Words like "investment" have a different resonance than "price." An investment portends expansion, enhancement, and a bright future. Consider a monthly fitness program; rather than saying, "It's $99 a month," say, "For $99 a month, you're investing in your health and future wellbeing."

Immediately, the dialogue shifts, allowing clients to see the possibilities for their lives.

"Value" captures what clients stand to gain, but "cost" frequently implies a loss or sacrifice. When you talk about your offering, emphasise its special advantages. You may help buyers understand how your product fits with their goals and wants by phrasing it in terms of what it gives, such as "you'll feel more energised, confident, and healthier," which resonates significantly more than "it costs $100."

⚜

YOUR MESSAGE WILL HAVE a greater impact if you use detailed language. Saying "this product gives you premium quality without breaking the bank" is a better alternative to "this product is affordable." This shift emphasises both the quality and the experience that customers can expect. It shifts the focus of the discourse from limitations to empowerment. Words matter, and this specific phrase instills pride in having made a wise choice.

⚜

STORYTELLING THAT IS compelling is another effective tool. Tell a story that integrates the advantages into a realistic context instead of just listing features. Imagine having a renewed sense of energy and being prepared to take on the day every morning. "Our sleep aid isn't just a product; it's your ticket to revitalising your life." This hook draws readers in by enabling them to picture themselves benefiting from the product directly. The price disappears as they become a part of the narrative.

⚜

USING LANGUAGE TO PAINT a clear picture for clients helps them see the transformation. Use language that captures both the service and the journey they'll take, such as "30 days of guided transformation," rather than talking about a feature like "30 days of support." It's all about stirring up feelings in people, getting prospective clients to envision their lives not only as they are, but as they could be.

Participation is essential. Invite clients to discuss their needs and experiences rather than saturating them with technical jargon.

Employ language that promotes conversation. "What objectives do you have?'or "How can we assist you in realising your aspirations?'This allows clients to voice their desires and aligns your services with their vision, personalising the conversation. This change places them in control and promotes an understanding-based relationship.

Use the persuasive power of testimonies when talking about results. Allow happy clients to narrate their tales.

⚜

LET A CUSTOMER TELL you about their experience, rather of just saying, "Our product has helped many people." For example, "I struggled with my energy levels before I found this product." I now feel refreshed every morning when I get up!" This direct connection humanizes your offering and shows potential buyers the real-life impact it can have. It's not about the money; it's about the experience, the trip, and the success.

⚜

A FURTHER SUCCESSFUL tactic is to highlight exclusivity. Expressions such as "limited edition" or "exclusive offer" convey a feeling of exclusivity and urgency. This wording evokes feelings by implying that what you're presenting is special and something they shouldn't pass up. By presenting your product as an exceptional chance, you may change the topic of discussion from price to value.

Intriguing queries can also help you refocus.

Asking "What would it mean for you to reach your health objectives this year?" is a better question to ask instead of simply saying, "Our service costs $100.This turns the topic of conversation from money to goals in life. Consumers begin to consider what is feasible rather than what they must spend.

Developing a sense of community around your brand makes the value dialogue even more powerful. Present your products and services as a component of a greater movement rather than as simple transactions.

The phrase "Join thousands of satisfied customers who are transforming their lives with our unique approach" fosters a sense of community and motivates users to associate with like-minded individuals.

Use language that highlights how your product or service improves the lives of your customers. Phrases such as "unlock potential," "achieve peace of mind," or "discover freedom" encourage clients to consider the emotional benefits of their purchase.

⚬⚭⚬

BY FRAMING YOUR GOODS in terms of how they enhance lives, you strengthen the value concept by creating a bridge between yourself and your clients.

Make associations in the brains of your clients by using metaphors. Try stating "this tool is your secret weapon against chaos" instead of "this is a great tool for organisation." This language conjures up images that connect with customers' experiences. By framing your offer as a solution to their problems, it helps people understand the value that goes beyond the cost.

Being flexible is crucial while developing your messaging. Think about the words that your audience responds to. Different demographics resonate with different expressions. For a tech-savvy demographic, terms like "cutting-edge" and "innovative" might generate curiosity. For a more traditional audience, adjectives like "trustworthy" and "reliable" may carry greater weight. Making sure your language is appropriate for your audience will assist guarantee that your message is received well.

Remembering the impact of action words is important. The words "transform," "ignite," and "empower" connote velocity and energy. They prompt action and encourage prospective clients to think about what they should do next. Change your messaging from "you can buy our product" to "start your transformation today." This will motivate clients to act right away, rather than just think about it.

Adopting strong adjectives is important when stressing benefits. Words like "revolutionary," "game-changing," or "life-changing" exude enthusiasm and promise. They elevate your offering from the ordinary to the remarkable. By speaking in an engaging and motivating way, you grab people's attention and create a sense of urgency to take action.

Your encounters become even more human when you use a conversational tone. Communicate with clients as though you were having a sincere conversation with a buddy. Sayings such as "I understand; we've all been there" foster relatability and empathy.

Your audience will feel appreciated and understood if you use this tone, which will motivate them to interact with your message.

When appropriate, use humour. Use of humour can help your clients have an enjoyable encounter. Try using a humorous tone to describe it instead of a dry one, like this: "Consider this as your own personal superhero, ready to save you from mayhem!Humour allows clients to engage with your brand more personally by dismantling boundaries.

Techniques for Deflecting Price Conversations

Price-related discussions might divert attention from the true benefits that goods and services offer to consumers. When a consumer asks about price, it's a frequent mistake for the conversation to immediately turn to figures rather than the advantages and results that really set a service apart. It takes skill to navigate these conversations, a toolset of useful techniques to refocus attention on the special value proposition of what you have to offer.

Consider a situation where a client enquires about the cost at the outset. Take a minute to breathe and refocus the conversation rather than diving right into the numbers. First, without being condescending, answer their query. This strategy opens the door to exploring the true benefits that will resonate more deeply than any price tag while validating the customer's concern: "I know price is important, but let's talk about what this can do for you."

ONE EFFECTIVE STRATEGY is to ask questions that cause the attention to change. For example, enquire, "What obstacles do you want to overcome?or "What results are you hoping to attain?These questions help clients express their wants and requirements, which enables you to change the direction of the conversation. Focussing on their objectives can help you move from talking about prices to showing them how your product fits their dreams.

THIS STRATEGY CHANGES the engagement into a dialogue focussing on solutions rather than bucks.

Tell stories to reaffirm the worth of what you have to give. It gives a clear image when you tell stories of happy clients who have undergone transformation. For example, "Let me tell you about a client who struggled with this same issue. This kind of narrative captures attention and establishes an emotional connection, directing the conversation back to the powerful effects of your product instead of just its cost.

"After using our service, they achieved remarkable results." It gives your brand a more human touch and turns the conversation from pricing to the significant impact you can make.

Another effective method comes in promoting the competitive benefits of your offering. When asked about your pricing, change the subject to what makes you unique. "While there are cheaper options available, many don't offer the same level of quality and support we provide.

Our dedication to quality guarantees that you get more than just a product—you get an experience. This highlights the special qualities of your offering and presents it as an investment in quality, giving the buyer peace of mind.

Include pictures with your discussion. Use infographics, digital presentations, or brochures that prioritise features over costs whenever possible. Customers' attention is diverted from the expense to the value they will receive when they witness the impressive features and observable results displayed in front of them.

For example, show a visual comparison that features success stories, outcomes, or testimonials in instead of a price list. The idea that the experience much surpasses the initial outlay is reinforced by this tactic.

Deflecting discussions about prices can also be achieved by using a value-based pricing approach. Describe how the benefits and quality you offer your consumers are reflected in your pricing. "We've priced our products to give you the value and outcomes you deserve.

❧

BY FRAMING THE PRICE as a representation of the value provided, you maintain the attention where it belongs—on the things that are most important to the client. Consider it as an assurance that you'll reach your objectives.

Recognising and responding to customer complaints is a critical component of changing the discussion. When a client expresses a price-related worry, pause to show empathy. "I understand; it's always a factor." Then, turn slightly to show how your solution meets their particular requirements.

"Let me show you how this service has saved others both time and money in the long run." This empathic approach keeps the dialogue productive and enables for examination of how your solution might fit inside their budget while giving larger returns.

Reassure buyers via guarantees or trial periods. Offering a money-back guarantee or a trial phase decreases perceived risk and allows clients to experience the benefit firsthand before worrying about the expense. Because we are so sure you'll enjoy our product, we are providing a 30-day trial.

This strategy not only steers the conversation away from pricing but also presents your offering as a no-risk option. Experience the value without the stress.

Your choice of words can make a big difference in diverting conversational focus from costs. Make use of language that emphasises long-term advantages above immediate expenses.

For instance, "What's the benefit of accomplishing your objectives?invites clients to ponder over the wider picture and how your product might

improve their lives after they have made the initial purchase. Customers are able to recognise the possibility for return instead of just concentrating on the cost when they adopt this way of thinking, which cultivates an abundant mindset.

Have a curious response ready for enquiries about pricing. When a client queries, "What's the price?" respond with, "What's your budget?This opens the door to a discussion about their expectations and how your offering meets them.

⚜

WITH THE USE OF THIS tactic, you can demonstrate how your value offer may satisfy their demands while transforming a potentially hostile query into a cooperative conversation about what can be achieved.

Focus shifting may also involve instilling a sense of urgency. Instead of listing the cost, draw attention to special discounts or time-only advantages. "We're offering a special package that includes additional services at no extra charge for the next week."

THIS STRATEGY PUSHES the topic of price into the background by emphasising the value clients receive and the exceptional opportunity.

Developing a relationship with your clients will help you change the subject considerably. Developing a relationship with them helps you better understand their demands and adjust your responses accordingly. When you build a relationship based on authenticity, clients are more likely to talk about their goals instead of focussing only on the price.

This level of trust enables you to explain how your solution may facilitate their path, further turning the focus toward value.

Educating your staff to use these tactics improves your sales approach's overall efficacy. Organise role-playing games or seminars where team members practice rerouting enquiries about prices. Establishing a culture where value is valued above price gives your team confidence and gives them the resources they need to truly interact with clients.

FEEDBACK LOOPS ARE a useful tool for gathering insights from consumer interactions. Ask customers if they feel the item they bought is worth more than it cost after a transaction. Their observations can provide insightful advice on how to improve your messaging and future deflection tactics for price talks.

CHAPTER 3

BUILDING EMOTIONAL CONNECTIONS

Forging deep emotional bonds with clients elevates the sales process to a far higher plane. It all comes down to connecting on an emotional level, creating rapport, and earning trust. With this strategy, the focus shifts from a transactional relationship to one that has deeper resonance. Imagine entering a store where the salesperson is aware of not just your name but also your requirements, preferences, and goals.

This type of interaction fosters brand loyalty, converting sceptics into ardent supporters of your company.

Making decisions is heavily influenced by emotions. Individuals purchase feelings and experiences in addition to goods. A customer is more likely to make a purchase and come back for more encounters when they feel appreciated and understood. The way you interact with them is crucial. Pay close attention when a customer approaches you with a particular demand or difficulty.

What they say yields a wealth of information that can be used to construct a customised answer. "I recognise that you're trying to find a solution to your issue. Together, let's investigate how we might make that happen. This kind of language encourages cooperation and creates a connection that seems real and intimate.

One particularly effective method for fostering emotional bonds is storytelling. People adore stories because they are memorable, relatable, and captivating.

Give examples of how your product has improved the lives of others. This can be a client who overcame a protracted problem or someone who accomplished an objective they had previously given up on. These stories foster a sense of belonging among the patrons, giving them a sense of community. You're sharing a journey rather than just selling a product, and people can relate to that experience.

Knowing your clients' goals and reaching out to them is another effective tactic. What motivates them?

What aspirations or objectives do they have? Your offerings become far more than just transactions when you phrase them in terms of these objectives. Instead, they evolve into stepping stones toward personal fulfillment. Make sure you ask questions that help clients express their objectives. "What would it mean to you to achieve this?By associating your product's advantages with their goals, you enable them to imagine a future in which they thrive as a result of your provision.

◌∾∾

EMPATHY BUILDS A CONNECTION between you and your client. It involves genuinely appreciating their sentiments and emotions. Recognise a customer's hesitancy or frustration when they express it. "I see that you find this to be significant. This affirmation demonstrates your concern about their experience beyond the sale. Together, let's discover a workable solution. Customers are more likely to trust you and establish a deeper relationship when they feel heard and understood.

◌∾∾

CUSTOMISATION STRENGTHENS the emotional connection you're forming. Using a customer's name in conversation, remembering their previous encounters, and noting their preferences all convey that they matter. Customers value it when companies go above and above to make them feel unique. It's similar to having a personal concierge as opposed to a salesperson. This feeling of individuality encourages loyalty, producing a partnership that lives on mutual respect and understanding.

◌∾∾

EMOTIONAL RELATIONSHIPS are largely established by creating a welcoming environment. Your interactions with customers can have a big impact on how they feel and what they experience. Think of things like the décor, music, and lighting. Having a cosy and welcoming environment will help clients feel more comfortable and willing to interact with you. Customers are more inclined to communicate their needs and desires when they are at ease, which sparks deeper exchanges and relationships.

Enhancing the connection can also be achieved by integrating emotional triggers into your marketing efforts. Creating emotional stories, language, and imagery for your customers makes it easier for them to picture themselves reaping the rewards of your product. Consider commercials that highlight true tales of change, achievement, or triumphing over adversity. Customers feel more emotionally connected to those events and are more likely to take action when they recognise themselves in them.

Additionally, building a community around your brand strengthens the emotional connection. Provide forums where clients can discuss their struggles, triumphs, and experiences. Encouraging discourse among customers through social media, forums, or events can foster a sense of community and increase their emotional bond with your company. They start to view you as a community that encourages and supports its members rather than just as a company.

Customer loyalty is fuelled by this sense of belonging, which also turns them into brand ambassadors.

It's critical to maintain relationships after the transaction. It demonstrates your concern for them after the sale by following up to find out how they're like their purchase and whether they need any additional help. Encouraging recurring business with special offers or handwritten thank-you notes strengthens the emotional bond. It's about building enduring connections based on gratitude and trust, not just closing the deal.

Feedback loops are a great tool for fostering these relationships. Get input from customers on a regular basis to learn about their thoughts and emotions. This allows you to better customise your services to match their changing wants while also demonstrating your appreciation for their feedback. Customers' emotional commitment in your brand is increased when they see that their opinions are valued.

⚬✲✲⚬

BY WORKING TOGETHER in this fashion, a partnership is cultivated instead of the conventional customer-business relationship.

Use body language to your advantage when interacting with others. Words frequently fall short of expressing the feelings that nonverbal signs do. To establish a relationship, keep eye contact, make open gestures, and mimic the customer's body language. Your behaviours convey warmth and approachability, which builds comfort and trust and lets the conversation flow easily.

Resolving client issues quickly is crucial to preserving emotional bonds. When problems emerge, act quickly and empathetically. Prove to clients that you care about their happiness. "I know this is frustrating; let's work together to resolve this." This strategy not only eases the immediate worry but also builds stronger relationships by making clients feel taken care of during trying times.

Understanding Customer Needs

Recognising the needs of the consumer turns the sales process from a transactional exchange into a genuine partnership. It's all about probing deeper, getting beyond surface-level queries, and tapping into the true motivations that drive purchases. Active listening and sincere curiosity are necessary for this procedure to create a welcoming atmosphere where clients feel at ease discussing their experiences.

Making a meaningful connection is more important than merely gathering data.

Take part in meaningful conversations first. Adopt an open communication strategy that encourages clients to express themselves, as opposed to using predetermined questions. For example, rather than enquiring, "What are you looking for? Attempt asking, "What brings you here today? Customers are able to discuss their goals and motives in a more natural way thanks to this small change.

They are more inclined to disclose their underlying wants when they feel that you are interested in their story.

An important part of this process is body language. A welcome environment is created by keeping eye contact and making open gestures. Lean in slightly to demonstrate attentiveness, and nod in recognition to suggest understanding. Customers are encouraged to open up more by these nonverbal cues, which let them know that their words count.

Customers are more likely to share the real factors behind their decisions when they feel heard and noticed.

Peeling back the layers of comprehension requires asking follow-up questions. When a client expresses a need, answer with questions that make them think more deeply. For instance, you could enquire, "What does convenience mean to you? " if someone expresses desiring a product for convenience." or "How would you see this product being used in your life?

BY ASKING MORE SPECIFIC questions, you can get a better understanding of your clients' needs and how your products can meet them.

Understanding client wants also requires an understanding of pain issues. These issues are generally the driving reason behind a purchase choice. Customers' problems and frustrations can be actively heard, and you can offer your product as a solution. Express empathy by validating their experiences and demonstrating your understanding of their difficulties. "You're heard. That has to be annoying.

This method turns a straightforward transaction into a cooperative effort centred on problem-solving. Let's see how we might help.

Making use of client feedback might help you better understand what people need. Solicit feedback not just after a purchase but during the process. Talk with customers about their expectations, preferences, and experiences. Direct talks, social media contacts, and polls can all be used for this. Make the most of this insightful data to improve your products and services and get them closer to what your clients actually desire. Customers become more loyal when they perceive that you are paying attention and making adjustments.

A layer of personalisation is added to your approach by developing personas or profiles based on client insights. You can customise your communication strategy by classifying your clients according to shared needs and behaviours. This aids in creating messages that strongly connect with particular audience segments. For example, while interacting with a group that is looking for eco-friendly solutions, you might emphasise the product's sustainability features. This tailored communication generates a sense of understanding and relevance.

Comprehending the demands of customers entails acknowledging the emotional aspects involved. Emotions frequently influence people's decisions; reasoning is not the only factor in decision-making. Recognise the emotions concealed in the words. Take advantage of a customer's excitement if they show it regarding a possible purchase. "You seem to be quite passionate about this.

What about it most intrigues you? This method strengthens their emotional bond with the product while also identifying their demands.

To learn more, watch how your consumers behave and what patterns they follow. Observe their interactions, both online and off, with your brand. Are there any recurring queries or worries? By examining these behaviours, patterns that indicate underlying requirements can be found.

⚜

FOR INSTANCE, IF A large number of clients regularly ask for a particular feature, that can point to a larger need. Use this knowledge to inform your communication strategy, focusing on those components that resonate best.

Using storytelling in your encounters can assist clients in expressing their wants. Invite them to talk about their experiences using your service or product. "Can you tell me about a time when you faced a challenge that our product could help with?

These tales build an emotional bond that fortifies your relationship in addition to offering insightful information. When customers feel themselves represented in your offers, they become more engaged.

Creating an environment of trust fosters open communication. Customers are more inclined to communicate their true requirements and desires when they are at ease. Be open and honest about your services, costs, and procedures to foster confidence.

⚜

BEING TRUTHFUL ABOUT your capabilities helps others trust that you are looking out for their best interests. For customers to feel free to express their opinions, this trust is essential.

Making use of technology can also help you better understand what your customers require. Tools for customer relationship management (CRM) let you keep track of contacts, preferences, and comments throughout time. Examine this data to find trends and foresee need in the future.

For instance, if a consumer repeatedly returns for comparable things, you can proactively propose relevant items that fit with their interests. Customers connect with this degree of personalisation because it conveys a sense of attentiveness.

It is essential to empower your team to meaningfully interact with customers. Teach your salespeople to focus on the needs of the consumer. Urge them to pose insightful queries and pay close attention to their answers.

They can become more confident in identifying wants and desires by participating in role-playing scenarios. Your staff may effectively steer conversations towards deeper insights when they possess the necessary abilities.

Acknowledge how crucial timing is in these exchanges. There's a thin line separating attentiveness from pestering clients with enquiries. Determine how comfortable they are, then modify your strategy accordingly. While some clients would value a straight and concentrated talk, others might prefer a more casual exchange.

Being flexible enables you to meet clients where they are, resulting in a more positive interaction.

The way that clients convey their wants is greatly influenced by the physical surroundings. Open communication is fostered by a welcoming and orderly environment. When interacting with customers, take into account design, lighting, and even background music. They feel more comfortable in a welcoming environment, which facilitates more open communication.

Customers are more inclined to openly express their opinions when they are at ease.

By applying social listening techniques, you can gain a deeper comprehension of the demands of your customers. Keep an eye on discussions about your brand on internet and social media channels. Observe debates, comments, and feedback pertaining to your sector. This outside perspective offers a comprehensive understanding of the preferences and needs of the customer.

Storytelling as a Value Tool

Storytelling has a special power; it can create stories that turn products from things to treasured memories. It evokes feelings beyond the transactional by drawing clients into a universe in which they can identify with the story. As tales come to life, people's perspectives are altered, which affects how consumers perceive value.

Imagine a little bakery that has been in the family for many generations. Rather than only promoting pastries, the bakery tells the genesis narrative, which includes a grandmother's family recipe, the delight of making together, and the custom of gathering the community around freshly baked bread. This story entices buyers by elevating a basic loaf to a representation of cosiness, reminiscence, and warmth. They savour the bread's history together with its flavour as they bite into a chunk.

Think of a tech business introducing a new device. Instead of concentrating just on the technical details, they tell a tale about how this gadget changed someone's life.

Maybe it helped a student learn how to code through interactive applications, or it helped a mother bond with her kids through games they played together. Through highlighting these practical effects, the business offers a value that goes beyond features. The buyer begins to visualise how this gadget could enrich their own life, generating an emotional tie that price tags can't touch.

Establishing a personal connection between the brand and the client is facilitated by using storytelling as a value mechanism.

Customers will find it easier to identify with the story as it establishes relatability. Customers are motivated when a clothing business tells tales of people who overcome obstacles and wear their clothes as symbols of fortitude. Their perspective is altered by this feeling of empowerment, and they become anxious to wear the brand as a badge of honour rather than just a piece of apparel.

Think about the resonance that good storytelling may have with a variety of audiences.

⌒⟨⟩⌒

TESTIMONIALS FROM FAMILIES who made treasured travel memories could be displayed by a travel business. Rather than advertising a trip package, they feature kids laughing while making sandcastles or couples enjoying candlelight meals while the sun sets. Customers are moved by this striking imagery, which makes them want to plan a vacation that promises to provide them comparable delights and inspires them to picture their own travels.

⌒⟨⟩⌒

AUTHENTICITY IS ALSO fostered by the craft of storytelling. Today's consumers yearn for real relationships with brands. Companies foster trust by sharing anecdotes based on actual experiences. A cosmetics brand might showcase a customer's journey of self-discovery, illustrating how their products played a role in improving confidence. Customers can relate to the brand on a personal level thanks to this narrative's ability to build an emotional bridge.

⌒⟨⟩⌒

THEY ARE COMPELLED to participate more fully because they see behind the label and recognise how it affects actual lives.

In order to use storytelling effectively, brands need to focus on being relatable. Connection is built by sharing setbacks and victories that speak to their intended audience. A fitness brand can motivate people going through similar experiences by sharing the story of one of its customers who overcame challenges to reach their health goals.

⌒⟨⟩⌒

THE BRAND ENCOURAGES customers to embrace the items that enabled their journey by putting them in the role of the hero and reinforcing the idea that success is achievable.

Storytelling with images increases the effect even more. Words alone are unable to elicit the same feelings as visuals or movies. A furniture firm might display images of happy families sharing meals and making memories around the dining table, complete with resounding laughing.

$$\sim\!\!\infty\!\!\sim$$

CUSTOMERS ARE DRAWN into the experience by these images, which let them see how those same things would improve their own lives. People emotionally connect with things when they see happiness linked with them, which raises the perceived value above that of simple furniture.

Making use of social media platforms is a great way to share stories. Using compelling stories to engage customers can start conversations and promote a sense of community.

Encourage customers to share their stories concerning your products. These sincere endorsements function as engrossing tales that foster a feeling of community. Customers become devoted to a company and brand ambassadors when they recognise themselves in other people's experiences.

A distinctive examination of worth is also made possible by skilful storytelling. Rather than basing a product's value primarily on its cost, marketers might highlight the product's long-term advantages and emotional benefits.

A company that sells gardening tools might share the narrative of a client who created a calm haven in their backyard and enjoyed peaceful moments with their loved ones. The happiness and tranquilly it brings about become more valuable than any amount of money.

Stories are another tool that brands may use to tell consumers about what they have to offer. A health food company might describe how it goes about obtaining ingredients from nearby farms while highlighting environmentally friendly methods.

Customers are informed about the product's quality by this narrative, which also demonstrates the company's dedication to moral business conduct. Customers begin to appreciate the effort behind the scenes, making them more likely to buy products that correspond with their values.

Because storytelling is so flexible, marketers can modify their messaging to fit different situations. Storytelling components can be used to seasonal ads to establish a sense of urgency and connection.

$$\sim\!\!\infty\!\!\sim$$

A CAMPAIGN WITH A CHRISTMAS theme may intertwine stories about family get-togethers to highlight the notion that the company's goods contribute to the creation of treasured memories. When products are linked to significant events, consumers are captivated and want to be a part of the narrative.

Storytelling is a timeless method that continues to engage clients profoundly even as the marketplace changes. It turns routine transactions into emotionally charged, meaningful events.

By utilising storylines to their advantage, marketers can change the focus of the conversation from price to value, which will increase customer loyalty and create enduring bonds.

Encouraging creativity within the workplace can also help storytelling efforts. Authenticity is fostered by giving team members the freedom to talk about their individual interactions with the brand. These tales can be incorporated into marketing collateral to enhance and enrich the main plot.

CHAPTER 4
CREATING IRRESISTIBLE VALUE PROPOSITIONS

Authenticity, relatability, and undeniable benefits must all be woven together to create value propositions that grab attention. It's more important to convey the core of what makes an offering genuinely alluring than just enumerating features or prices. Imagine a little company that offers experiences with every cup of coffee instead of just selling it.

Rather than emphasising the price of a latte, they highlight the source of their beans, the enthusiasm of their neighbourhood roasters, and the cosy atmosphere of their café. Customers enter to experience more than simply a cup of coffee—they become part of a community, a narrative, and a happy moment.

Understanding your audience is the first step in creating value propositions that are compelling. Every consumer has a distinct set of requirements, preferences, and problems.

Spend some time engaging, listening, and showing empathy. A skincare company might change its strategy by paying attention to what customers have to say. Rather than just offering moisturisers, they develop a range made especially to fit different skin types, taking care of issues like irritation or dryness. Customers feel more connected to a brand when they see that their particular requirements have been taken into consideration, which increases the attraction of the brand's goods.

USING LANGUAGE THAT resonates also plays a key role in communicating value. Clarity is promoted by avoiding jargon and complex terminology. For instance, a fitness brand can communicate its objective as follows: "We're here to help you feel stronger and more confident." This kind of communication draws clients in and harmonises the firm's values with those of potential customers. Clear and understandable messaging foster curiosity and trust, which motivates further investigation of the brand's products.

Design and imagery significantly improve value propositions. A product's presentation should be a narrative unto itself. Consider a high-end candle company that presents its goods in beautiful, reusable packaging. Every candle becomes into a work of art rather than just a source of smell or light. The careful design and attention to detail increase its status, making clients ready to invest. Perceived value rises dramatically when a product embodies the brand's values and story of excellence.

⟡

FURTHERMORE, INSTILLING a sense of urgency can make a solid offer seem enticing. A subscription box provider might introduce a limited-time offering that exhibits unique items crafted around a seasonal theme. Customers feel pressure to act quickly when they think they might lose out on something great. In addition to highlighting the value, this exclusivity creates excitement and increases the likelihood that customers will commit.

⟡

VALUE IDEAS ARE MADE more appealing through compelling narrative. Each product has a story, and telling that tale to others can leave a lasting impression. A tech firm may give an example of how one of its newest devices assisted a young entrepreneur in starting her own business. Prospective buyers can see how the product could help them by emphasising its personal impact. The object becomes an essential tool for success due to this link, transforming it from just another piece of technology.

⟡

A DIFFERENT TACTIC is to offer social proof. Case studies, reviews, and testimonies from customers speak for themselves. A house cleaning service may publish testimonies from happy customers explaining how hiring assistance improved their life. Prospective clients are more inclined to think about a service for themselves when they witness actual individuals using it. By fostering a climate of trust and dependability, this group endorsement strengthens the value offer without coming across as pushy.

Value propositions are more effective when they are personalised. Customers prefer offers suited to their unique interests. An online merchant can make product recommendations that match a customer's tastes by using the customer's browsing history and past purchases. A shop can increase the likelihood of a purchase by making the customer feel valued and showing that they understand their target by giving appropriate recommendations.

THIS PERSONAL TOUCH highlights a dedication to satisfying the individual's demands, strengthening the perceived value of the products.

Potential concerns are also addressed up front in a compelling value proposition. If a consumer hesitates because they're worried about product quality, a brand might proactively incorporate information regarding quality assurance or customer satisfaction assurances. By being transparent, this removes doubt and increases trust in the buying choice.

A travel company may provide thorough itineraries that show off how each component makes the trip better. Customers will be able to see the consideration that went into the offering, which will increase its persuasiveness.

Incorporating education into value propositions can further boost their attractiveness. A health food firm may provide online tools or workshops to inform consumers about nutrition. They increase the value of their products by presenting themselves as informed allies in the journeys of their clients.

This commitment to empowering others fosters a more meaningful connection, turning transactions into meaningful exchanges. Consumers value companies that care about their health and give them the resources they need to make wise decisions.

Seasonal marketing presents an additional chance to craft compelling value propositions. A clothing company can introduce a line that appeals to all age groups while reflecting the latest fashions.

THESE COLLECTIONS PROVIDE buyers with a sense of relevance by connecting them to certain occasions, such as summer vacations or holiday get-togethers. Customers are more likely to interact and make an investment when they perceive the product as smoothly fitting into their life.

Value proposals must take the emotional factor into consideration. Reaching out to clients' hopes, dreams, and desires can have a profound impact.

❧

A FINANCIAL PLANNING business may present its products and services as a way to help clients feel at ease and see themselves in a stable future. The value proposition is strengthened by this emotional connection, which also makes it more relatable to individuals. Customers are more inclined to accept the item completely when they are motivated.

Utilizing analytics and feedback loops ensures value offerings change with shifting consumer preferences. Brands may improve their messaging and products by remaining aware of their audience.

If a cosmetic brand observes rising interest in natural components, they might reorient their marketing efforts to promote these characteristics. They stay relevant and show that they are dedicated to providing genuine value by continuing to be flexible and adaptable.

Value propositions that incorporate sustainability appeal to today's environmentally sensitive customers. Prioritising environmentally friendly processes allows brands to demonstrate their environmental commitment and highlight how their products help create a more sustainable future. A brand of household cleaners might emphasise that it uses recyclable packaging and biodegradable components. The value of those products goes beyond the single purchase when consumers realise how their decisions affect the environment.

Value propositions can also be amplified through influencer collaboration. Influencers give brands legitimacy and authenticity, especially with younger consumers. Positive product experiences spread when well-known individuals talk about them.

Crafting Your Unique Selling Proposition (USP)

Creating a distinctive identity in the crowded market full of options can be likened to meandering through a thick forest. Every company claims to provide something distinctive, but how can you make sure your message shines? The first step is identifying your unique selling proposition (USP), or what makes you stand out. Finding your USP is a journey that takes time and includes introspection, research, and a thorough comprehension of your target market.

Making an honest evaluation of your contributions is the first step. Step back and think about what makes you different from the competition. Is it the creative design of your product? Maybe the outstanding customer service is what keeps customers coming back for more. Perhaps the solution lies in your brand's history and backstory. Your USP's core is made up of all these components.

Getting feedback from your clients is quite valuable. Reach out and listen intently to their experiences and feedback.

What about your offerings do they like best? Which issues do you resolve on their behalf? Sometimes, customers express admiration for areas of your business that you may ignore. Maybe they value the attention you take in your production procedures or the way you customise services for them. Each bit of criticism adds a layer to your understanding, helping you build a message that connects.

One very useful instrument in this approach is market research. Examine the surroundings and determine who your rivals are.

What are they endorsing? Which messaging do they think their audience will connect with? It's important to forge your own path, but understanding what other people find impressive might help you find areas where your own talents come through. It's important to note not only what they say but also how they say it. What are their tonalities? Which feelings do they engage with? You can use this analysis to place your voice in a way that sounds inviting and new.

WHEN YOU START OUTLINING your USPs, think about emphasising the advantages above the features. Customers relate more deeply to the value your product adds to their lives than they do to the fact that it is constructed of premium materials. For instance, a sustainable clothing company might highlight not just the eco-friendly fibres utilised but the larger benefit of adopting ecologically responsible decisions. By connecting with the values of the clients, this strategy forges a link that goes beyond simple business dealings.

Another key part involves storytelling. Every company has a narrative, and integrating yours into the fabric of your USP increases your relationship with your audience. Talk about the steps you took to build your brand, the difficulties you encountered, and the successes you were proud of. These narratives have the power to fervently advocate for a brand, whether it's a touching account of a family recipe or the commitment to creating handcrafted goods.

YOUR DISTINCTIVE MESSAGE should be supported by visual components. Your USP can be expressed visually through your branding, packaging, and marketing materials without using words. Vibrant hues, original designs, and captivating imagery convey your brand's essence. Think about how the packaging of a gourmet snack could build excitement even before the first taste. Your core values are reaffirmed and made memorable by this visual language.

SIMPLICITY AND CLARITY are necessary for USP articulation. While it may be tempting to include as much detail as you can, it is more beneficial to communicate your point in its most basic form. A brief mission statement or slogan can capture your soul in an understandable manner. This simplicity increases the likelihood that clients will remember you in a plethora of options by helping them quickly understand your distinct value.

YOU MAY WANT TO TEST your USP on a small sample of friends or reliable clients. Collect input and watch how they respond. Do they find it intriguing? Do they show an interest in finding out more? Your message can be improved and made more relatable to the people you want to reach with the help of this early validation.

The next stage is to integrate your USP across all communication channels after you've determined and crafted it. Make sure your distinctive points come through in everything you write, including social media postings and website material. Customers may readily make the connections between your brand and this cohesive strategy, which strengthens it. Having your USP in every interaction helps build familiarity and trust and helps lead potential clients from awareness to purchase.

Always remember to embrace your authenticity when crafting your USP. Customers desire for real relationships in a world full with replicas. Communicate with your personality coming through, and don't be scared to be vulnerable.

Customers can relate to you on a personal level when you share your struggles and accomplishments, forging an emotional connection that encourages loyalty.

It takes constant evolution to establish your unique selling point. You shouldn't stand still since the market never does. Keep an eye out for new competitors, evolving trends, and shifting consumer preferences. Adaptation is about refining your identity to fit the changing environment, not about losing your essential self.

Regularly examine your USP to ensure it corresponds with your business goals and connects with your audience.

Your understanding of competition changes as you improve your USP. Consider it as a benchmark instead than a barrier. Examine what works for others, then add your unique flavour to make your offering stand out. This kind of thinking fosters teamwork rather than hostile rivalry, which enables you to develop in a fast-paced setting.

THE INFLUENCE OF A great USP extends beyond initial consumer interactions. It creates the foundation for more meaningful connections. Customers feel more connected and appreciated when they know what makes you different. This relationship fosters advocacy and brand loyalty, as pleased consumers turn become your most vociferous advocates. They naturally aid in word-of-mouth communication by sharing their experiences with friends and family.

⸎

SOCIAL MEDIA MAGNIFIES voices in the digital world, and your USP may become a rallying cry. Creating interesting content that draws attention to your special talents can spark conversations, shares, and recommendations with a far larger audience than just your immediate followers. The sincerity of your message and the connections you make are what fuel this organic growth.

Delivering Value Beyond the Transaction

Every client connection has the opportunity to build enduring relationships, and the magic emerges when a transaction becomes more than just a transaction. The consumer journey doesn't stop at the register when they make a purchase. Rather, it provides access to a plethora of chances for engagement, loyalty, and connection that can propel your business to unprecedented heights.

LET'S CONSIDER WHAT transpires following a transaction first. This is the point at which a lot of firms miss a huge opportunity. Consider the effect of sending a personalised message to customers to express gratitude for their purchase. Amidst a sea of automatic responses, it can feel like a breath of fresh air. A brief note of sincere gratitude can go a long way towards fostering a positive relationship that lasts long after the first transaction.

WHEN IT COMES TO BUILDING a good rapport and getting consumers to come back, this gesture can make all the difference.

Now, consider after-sales service. After the product is delivered, support is still required; it is a continuous effort. Superior post-purchase support fosters trust by giving resources for enhanced product utilisation, troubleshooting assistance, and answer to queries. When customers feel helped, they are more inclined to come back.

CREATE A SYSTEM THAT makes it simple for customers to contact you by phone, email, or chat. Being approachable conveys your appreciation for their experience and your dedication to ensuring their happiness.

Programs for loyalty show up as yet another effective way to add value. These initiatives foster a sense of community in addition to rewarding consumers for their continued business. Envision a rewards program that provides access to unique events, discounts on subsequent purchases, and exclusive experiences in addition to points.

It creates an interesting and captivating experience out of an ordinary shopping trip. Consumers start to view the brand as a lifestyle option rather than just a store. They return not only for the savings but also for the sense of community you've created, which gives them a sense of belonging as they accrue awards.

Additionally, engagement methods are essential to this process. Maintaining a constant presence on social media and in newsletters helps consumers remember your brand.

Provide advice, product updates, or even behind-the-scenes looks at the working culture of your business. Customers are invited into your environment and given a sense of participation by your transparency. Invite them to write reviews, testimonials, or post on social media about their interactions with your products. By showcasing client success stories, you may foster a feeling of collective pride in your business.

<hr />

DON'T UNDERESTIMATE the influence of instructional materials. Providing product-related seminars, lessons, or guidelines can greatly improve the client experience. Customers value their purchases more when they feel prepared to get the most out of them. This educational component indicates you care about their long-term enjoyment and want them to succeed with your services. Once you establish your brand as a useful resource, you can maintain client engagement even beyond the transaction.

<hr />

CUSTOMISATION OFFERS an additional depth layer. Customise experiences by leveraging data and customer insights. For example, send personalized suggestions based on previous purchases or tailor marketing efforts to specific interests. Customers love feeling acknowledged as individuals rather than just numbers in a database. This strategy improves relationships and may boost sales and loyalty.

Adding consumer input to your processes is another good way to deliver value over time.

Customers feel a sense of ownership over your business when they see that you value and act upon their opinions. Provide channels for them to express opinions and ideas, such as social media or polls. Recognising their input demonstrates your awareness of their requirements and flexibility.

Developing a community around your business increases consumer interaction even more. Organise events where clients may engage with you and your staff in person or electronically.

Customers can develop relationships and share their stories at these get-togethers. Customers feel more a part of your brand when they have a sense of community. Whether it's through live events, social media groups, or online forums, creating this atmosphere encourages active participation from customers.

It is imperative that the significance of trust be emphasised. When customers trust your brand, they are more likely to stick with you. It takes effort to build this trust, but it can be maintained by being open and honest about procedures, keeping promises, and communicating consistently. For example, if there's an issue with a product, talk freely about it and give remedies. Stronger relationships result from this honesty's ability to establish credibility.

Loyal consumers may also benefit from exclusive offers or first access to new products. These promotions provide clients a feeling of exclusivity and appreciation. Because of the additional care customers receive in addition to the items, they are more inclined to come back.

Using narrative to its fullest potential in your communications gives your brand life. Talk about the people that went into making your products, the journey they took, and the principles you uphold. Consumers relate to stories that touch them on an emotional level, which increases brand recall. A story that shares the ideals of your audience makes them feel devoted and included.

Taking a step further, try engaging with influencers or brand advocates who agree with your values.

These alliances have the power to increase your credibility and reach. Influencers lend a human touch to your brand by sharing their real-life stories.

Customers are more likely to interact with and believe in your brand when they witness actual people taking use of your goods.

Creating an emotional bond with clients is essential to converting them into devoted lifelong supporters. When consumers truly connect with your brand, they turn into brand ambassadors who tell others about their great experiences.

Word-of-mouth advertising like this can greatly increase your reach by attracting new clients who are ready to interact with your products.

Developing iconic experiences for your brand can help increase client loyalty. These small actions, like a handwritten letter of appreciation, a surprise present with purchase, or a special discount on their birthday, leave a lasting impression. Customers remember the extra mile you went, and that memory turns into loyalty.

⟿⟾

IT'S CRITICAL TO REMAIN current. Watch for developments in technology and trends that have the potential to improve your clientele's experience. Whether it's harnessing social media platforms for engagement or employing chatbots for instant customer assistance, keeping up with the changing landscape is essential to keeping your brand at the forefront of consumers' minds.

CHAPTER 5

HANDLING PRICE OBJECTIONS WITH CONFIDENCE

Managing pricing objections is similar to balancing the requirement to communicate value with the need to make sure the customer feels heard and understood. When someone expresses financial problems, it's critical to enter the conversation with confidence and understanding. Every criticism is a doorway, beckoning you to interact, comprehend, and assist the client in seeing the genuine value of what you have to provide.

Imagine that a prospective client shows reluctance regarding your pricing. Rather than immediately going into defence mode, pause to breathe and pay attention. Each and every objection contains a secret meaning, a window into the customer's worldview. Maybe they are comparing costs, are unsure about the investment, or just want to know exactly what they will be getting in return.

ACTIVE LISTENING TURNS objections into fruitful dialogue that lets you address their particular problems with your response.

Here, empathy is the main player. Respect their emotions and give credence to their worries. A tone of understanding and assurance is established by statements like "I understand where you're coming from" or "It's completely normal to have questions about pricing."

This small change opens the door to a more in-depth conversation by fostering an atmosphere where customers feel comfortable sharing more about their reservations.

It's time to shift the topic of the conversation to value once you've created rapport. Focus the conversation on the advantages of your offering rather than just the cost. Give a clear explanation of how your good or service will improve their life, assist them reach their objectives, or solve their problems.

⬥

EMPLOY NARRATIVE TECHNIQUES to provide concrete instances of how other people have profited from your products or services, emphasising outcomes that are in line with the needs of your target audience.

Think of using the "feel, felt, found" approach. This age-old tactic draws the client into a shared experience. Begin by expressing empathy ("I understand how you feel"), then give a sympathetic anecdote about another customer who encountered similar problems ("Others have felt the same way").

Lastly, point them in the direction of the favourable result that resulted from their choice to proceed ("What they found was that the value far outweighed the initial hesitation"). This method reassures the customer by humanising the conversation and offering a gripping story.

Be ready to directly answer any objections that are raised. Consumers could have concerns about the product's quality, its guarantee, or the assistance it comes with. Arm yourself with credible proof to support your views, such as statistics, testimonies, or case studies.

Possessing information will make you seem confident and comfort the buyer that they are making a well-informed choice.

Adding comparisons can also aid in making value more clear. Comparing your price to that of your competitors can help clients feel more at ease when they are unsure about it. Rather of just saying that your product is better, show how the extra features or advantages make the price worthwhile. This is about emphasising the distinctive qualities that make your offering stand out, not about denigrating competitors. Consumers value openness and are able to make better decisions when they have a clearer understanding of the situation.

Occasionally, the topic of discussion may turn to different approaches. A client may indicate interest in a less costly choice. This might be a crucial moment. Instead of just giving them a discount, find out more about their needs. Find out their goals and priorities by probing them with questions. This inquiry offers a chance to better present your offering while also showcasing your dedication to identifying the best answer. Perhaps the higher-priced option has features that correspond better with their aims, which you should emphasize to make the value very evident.

In this procedure, transparency is crucial. Don't be afraid to share any justifications for your pricing, such as greater customer service, craftsmanship, or materials. Clients value being informed about their investments. They are more inclined to view the price as reasonable rather than exorbitant if they find merit in your justification.

Making things urgent can also affect how decisions are made. Once clients are aware of the value, you can motivate them to take action by emphasising any limited-time offers or time-sensitive promotions. It's important to gently guide them towards a conclusion that is in line with their needs and goals rather than exerting pressure on them.

Keep in mind that every consumer is different, and their decisions are influenced by their own experiences and situations. Adapting your answers to the particular situation helps strengthen your bond.

Consider their past encounters with your brand, their past purchases, and the preferences they have stated. This meticulous attention to detail demonstrates your value for them as people, not just as customers.

All during the chat, keep your stance confident. Self-assurance generates trust. Your tone, body language, and word choice all show how much you value what you're delivering. When customers perceive your conviction, they are more inclined to react favourably. But this assurance must never give way to conceit.

Remain sensible, personable, and willing to communicate.

When there's tension, body language counts. Collaboration can be fostered by keeping eye contact, making open movements, and matching the customer's energy. Nonverbal clues reaffirm your dedication to comprehending and assisting them with their worries. The whole experience is improved by this tiny link, which makes it seem less transactional and more like a partnership.

WATCH FOR SYMPTOMS of reluctance or confusion as the talk goes on. Ask the customer to express their opinion if they seem to be unsure. Enquiries such as "What's preventing you?or "What are your thoughts on the topics we covered?"Promote conversation. This gives you the opportunity to address any unanswered questions and opens up the conversation.

Encouraging decision-making might also involve offering a trial or a guarantee.

CUSTOMERS CAN EXPERIENCE the benefit without feeling pressured to commit by using a satisfaction guarantee, which helps allay concerns about making the wrong decision. This guarantee shows your faith in the item and your dedication to making sure they are satisfied.

Techniques for Addressing Price Concerns

Handling consumer price issues might be likened to meandering through a labyrinth of turns and turns, with obstacles lurking around every corner. The trick is this, though: each obstacle presents a chance to emphasise the genuine worth of what you have to give. When a consumer brings up price, it's not the end of the conversation; rather, it's an opportunity to refocus it on the advantages that make your product or service stand out from the competitors.

One's natural response to concerns expressed by clients regarding affordability or comparative pricing may be to immediately defend the price. Instead, inhale and change your attention. Begin by paying attention. Respond to their worries in a way that demonstrates your appreciation for their viewpoint. This first action establishes the foundation for a meaningful conversation. By expressing your understanding of their emotions, such as "I know price is a concern," you open up a dialogue and foster a closer bond.

Moving the debate back towards value is crucial at this stage. Direct the conversation towards the advantages that speak to the requirements of the consumer rather than getting bogged down in the statistics. Present your good or service as a fix rather than a cost. Emphasise particular qualities that deal with their particular problems. For example, highlight the product's quality and longevity if they're concerned about a higher price.

TELL THE TALES OF CONTENTED clients who reaped long-term rewards, demonstrating the concrete impact your product has had on their life.

Regarding typical criticisms such as "It's too expensive," see this as a chance to highlight the return on investment. Compare the short-term costs to the long-term gains. Maybe your product improves their overall experience by saving them money or time in the long term. Make use of analogies that help to clarify the value. Show how investing a bit more money up front can result in substantial savings or better results over time. This rephrasing encourages the buyer to consider the benefits rather than focussing only on the cost.

Customers may occasionally voice complaints about receiving inadequate value for their money. In these situations, return attention to their needs. To find out what they're especially looking for, ask open-ended questions. By being aware of their priorities, you can adjust your response such that the advantages of your product meet their needs.

⟨∞⟩

THIS INDIVIDUALISED approach creates a sense of connection while also assisting in addressing their difficulties.

Storytelling can be a very useful tactic in this situation. Telling tales of former clients who were first dubious about their choice but ended up being happy about it helps build a compelling story. This approach emphasises that the price is just a means to an end—satisfaction and peace of mind—while appealing to the emotional component of buying.

⟨∞⟩

COMPARISONS TO COMPETITORS are a common topic of discussion in price complaints. When a client brings up a less expensive choice elsewhere, avoid criticising the other business. Instead, take advantage of this to emphasise what makes your product special. Talk about the extra features or first-rate customer support that make the price difference worthwhile. Clients value integrity and openness; a tactful analogy might increase your trustworthiness.

⟨∞⟩

YOU NEED TO BE CAUTIOUS if buyers tell you that they can't afford your product. Recognise their worries without passing judgement on them. Provide adaptable options, like financing or payment plans, that can be more appropriate for their circumstances. These substitutes show your dedication to meeting their demands by indicating that you're interested in assisting them in gaining access to the value you provide.

WHEN CLIENTS DOUBT the value of what you're providing, present case studies and testimonials that demonstrate actual outcomes. The perceived worth of your product increases when prospective customers learn about the positive changes it has made in other people's lives or businesses. Their confidence in their choice is increased by the strong motivating effect of this social proof.

Adding a trial period or money-back guarantee is another smart move.

OFFERING A METHOD FOR clients to enjoy the value without the risk promotes a sense of security. It reduces obstacles to access, allowing them to check out your goods or service before committing entirely. This tactic builds trust while demonstrating your assurance in your abilities. Customers feel more in control of their decision-making when they are aware of their possibilities.

It's crucial to keep your composure and cool throughout this process. Your tone and body language should convey approachability and confidence when worries about price are raised. Assure them that you are available to assist them in making their decision and that it is quite normal to have questions. This creates a more laid-back environment that facilitates their ability to communicate their ideas and emotions.

Put more effort on developing a friendship than a transaction. Maintaining contact after the sale might allay worries down the road and show how valuable you are to the company.

FREQUENT CHECK-INS, customised communications, or special deals for devoted clients can help them feel valued and appreciated. This strategy encourages consumers to tell others about their excellent experiences while also aiding in client retention.

Training Your Team to Talk Value

The skill of effectively expressing value is crucial in the fast-paced world of sales. Stories, connections, and sincere bonds are more important than just numbers when it comes to turning a one-time encounter into an enduring friendship. Teams that possess the ability to communicate value successfully boost client experiences, transforming routine transactions into significant ones.

THIS FLEXIBLE STRATEGY creates an environment where building relationships with customers comes before talking about prices.

Consider a sales team that gets great satisfaction from comprehending the subtleties of their clients' wants. Instead of just trying to sell a product, every conversation becomes a chance to establish rapport. Employers need to make training investments in order to foster this culture. Training shouldn't be a box to check off; it needs to be an engaging journey that empowers team members with the knowledge and abilities to convey value in a relatable manner.

The first step in creating a training program is to concentrate on the principles of good communication. Workers should be taught the value of active listening, which entails grasping the underlying goals and concerns in addition to only hearing what is being said. When a team listens intently, they can carefully answer and establish a personal connection with the customers. Role-playing games can make this idea come to life.

Employees can practise expressing value and handling concerns without seeming scripted or robotic by modelling real-world circumstances.

It is revolutionary to use narrative in training sessions. Narratives give statistics and facts a human face, making abstract data more approachable. It is a good idea to encourage team members to offer personal anecdotes or client testimonials about how a specific product improved someone's life.

EMPLOYEES THAT ARE skilled at telling these stories create an emotional bond that is far more powerful than any price tag.

Training the team about the goods or services they represent is another essential component. Confidence comes from knowledge. Employees are better able to convey the worth of what they're selling when they are aware of its nuances and advantages. Frequent product knowledge training keep everyone informed and provide the team the confidence to easily handle concerns and respond to questions.

They are able to steer conversations away from cost and towards value thanks to this foundation of information.

The company's culture should be intertwined with values that are focused on the needs of the customer. At the top, there is a dedication to making customer relationships a priority. The way in which leaders interact with clients should go beyond debates about prices. Honouring team members who demonstrate this strategy helps to spread the word that fostering relationships is just as vital as hitting sales goals. Acknowledging those who invest the effort to comprehend and attend to the demands of their clients fosters an environment in which others are inspired to follow suit.

Establishing a feedback loop throughout the training procedure is equally important. Employees should be encouraged to consider their discussions after every encounter. What was effective? In what areas could they get better?

EMPLOYEES LEARN FROM one another when they share triumphs and setbacks as a team, which promotes development and cooperation. Over time, this continuous conversation about experiences helps them become more adept at conveying value.

Organising frequent workshops can also improve the team's competencies. Ask professionals in the field to discuss the latest developments, consumer trends, and efficient communication techniques.

These meetings offer new insights and motivation, rekindling passion and dedication to providing outstanding client experiences. Employees are more likely to adopt the mindset of valuing connections over transactions when they perceive that their professional development is appreciated.

The modern sales environment is heavily reliant on technology, and training programs ought to keep up with these developments.

⚜

IT'S CRITICAL TO PROVIDE staff with resources that improve customer engagement and expedite communication. Team members can monitor interactions and preferences, for instance, with the use of customer relationship management (CRM) systems. With this knowledge at their disposal, salespeople may customise their interactions and highlight value in a way that appeals to certain clients.

Developing success measurements that are value-centric is another useful strategy.

Instead of merely focusing on sales numbers, try assessing customer pleasure, loyalty, and engagement. The organisation promotes the idea that fostering connections is just as important as closing business by recognising staff members who excel in these areas. When workers witness that their endeavours to convey value are acknowledged and rewarded, they are more committed to preserving those connections.

⚜

AS VALUE COMMUNICATION becomes ingrained in the organisational culture, it permeates every encounter and has a cascading effect. When they interact with a workforce that actually cares about their requirements, customers notice the difference. Every exchange becomes a two-way discussion instead of a one-sided lecture about costs. This change fosters a level of client loyalty that goes well beyond a single transaction by encouraging customers to perceive the team as partners in their journey and to trust them.

Developing a culture of value communication helps boost customer loyalty and retention rates. Returning consumers are more likely to feel that their requirements are acknowledged and taken seriously. Moreover, delighted customers become brand champions, sharing their pleasant experiences with friends and family. Nothing can match the effectiveness of this natural word-of-mouth marketing strategy.

CHAPTER 6
MEASURING VALUE CREATION

Measuring the impact of value creation becomes a potent tool in the dynamic business landscape for assessing how well a firm satisfies the needs of its customers. Value measurement is a process that involves more than just math calculations; it involves distilling the essence of client experiences, assessing the level of engagement, and turning insights into practical plans.

Gaining an understanding of value assessment necessitates combining quantitative measurements with qualitative insights, fusing hard facts with consumer experiences and narratives.

At the heart of this measurement lies client feedback, a vital ingredient for assessing satisfaction. Interviews and surveys yield priceless insights into how clients assess the value they receive.

Businesses that make obtaining this input a top priority can access a multitude of insights that highlight both their areas of strength and opportunity for development. Something as basic as "How did our product impact your life?" may reveal a wealth of stories that firms can use to figure out what appeals to their target market.

Analytics of data is also very important. Tracking customer behavior through data such as purchase frequency, average order value, and customer lifetime value can reveal trends and patterns. This information clarifies how well the good or service satisfies the demands of the people who use it.

Businesses can use this data to determine which characteristics consumers value the most and which might use improvement. Businesses can concentrate on what really matters to their clients by using analytics to turn raw data into strategic decisions.

Another essential statistic in the value measurement toolbox is customer retention rates. High retention rates indicate that clients continue to find value in a business's offerings.

⊚⊗⊚

ON THE OTHER HAND, a high rate of client churn may suggest that they aren't getting the value they anticipated. Companies should make an effort to comprehend the factors influencing these KPIs and interact with departing consumers to learn more about their experiences. By identifying pain spots, firms can alter their services and communication methods, ensuring they resonate with present and new customers alike.

⊚⊗⊚

MAKING A VALUE PROPOSITION canvas can also completely transform the game. With this graphic tool, businesses can map out the requirements, wants, and anxieties of their customers alongside their goods. By matching products with what customers genuinely seek, firms can uncover gaps and possibilities for improvement. To stay ahead of the competition, teams can generate innovative ideas by brainstorming solutions that directly target client problem points.

⊚⊗⊚

THIS COLLABORATIVE strategy optimises value delivery, ensuring that organisations keep in sync with their consumers' shifting needs.

The Net Promoter Score (NPS) becomes a widely used metric to evaluate customer satisfaction and loyalty. Businesses can learn about customer sentiment by asking consumers if they would suggest the good or service to others. A high net promoter score (NPS) signifies that consumers see the brand as having good value and are eager to recommend it.

It also acts as a growth predictor; companies with a high promoter ratio typically see more notable organic growth. Companies can observe shifts in customer sentiment and modify their tactics by tracking variations in NPS over time.

Creating a community around the brand multiplies value creation as well. Using social media, forums, or events to interact with clients creates relationships that go beyond business. When clients experience a sense of belonging, their impression of value deepens.

Companies that help consumers make these connections can access a potent source of brand loyalty. Furthermore, comments received via community interactions might offer further understanding of the expectations and experiences of customers. By fostering a connection based on openness and trust, this conversation increases the perceived value that consumers place on the brand.

❧

EFFECTIVE VALUE COMMUNICATION training for teams is another aspect of measuring. When staff members are capable of communicating the advantages of goods or services, the customer experience is improved. Teams can stay in line with the changing environment by routinely reviewing their training programs. Organisations may foster a culture where every connection matters by putting a strong emphasis on customer engagement strategies and value communication.

Value-based KPI implementation is another successful strategy. Businesses can set up measurements that show customer loyalty and happiness rather than just income or volume of sales. Metrics that demonstrate the relationship between value delivery and customer behaviour include customer engagement score, repeat purchase rate, and referral rate. Decision-making is aided by these KPIs, which focus attention on projects that improve the customer experience.

❧

ENHANCING KNOWLEDGE of value creation can also be achieved through utilising customer success stories. Emphasising case studies and testimonials gives prospective clients a chance to view actual instances of how goods and services have improved the lives of others. This narrative strategy humanises the brand while reiterating the value proposition. Organisations establish credibility by showcasing the observable advantages enjoyed by current clients.

Metrics related to innovation offer an additional perspective on value generation. The degree to which innovations meet consumer wants can be determined by monitoring the adoption rates of new features or goods. An organisation may decide to give specific improvements top priority if they result in higher customer satisfaction or engagement. On the other hand, if new products don't catch on, the strategy needs to be reassessed. Maintaining flexibility and being receptive to client input encourages a continual improvement culture.

Making a customer journey map helps to visualise the whole process, from first awareness to interactions after the sale. This instrument facilitates the identification of touchpoints where clients get value and where difficulties arise. Organisations can optimise each stage of the customer experience and guarantee constant value delivery by having a comprehensive grasp of the whole spectrum.

The idea that customer pleasure counts at every stage of the relationship is reaffirmed by this all-encompassing strategy.

Assessing Customer Satisfaction

Measuring customer satisfaction turns into a game-changer in the fast-paced business environment by helping organisations realise how effective their value communication is. Through this method, teams may gain a tangible understanding of what connects with customers by turning hazy perceptions into actionable insights. An assortment of ways can be applied to analyse satisfaction, and each strategy gives a distinct lens through which to view the client experience.

Commence with surveys, a time-tested but potent instrument for obtaining input. These might be anything from concise, targeted surveys to in-depth evaluations. Asking questions about particular features of the good or service might assist identify areas that customers find most important. Establishing a safe and respected feedback environment is crucial. Encouraging clients to freely share their opinions can produce insightful information that informs future tactics.

Utilizing Net Promoter Score (NPS) is another excellent technique to assess customer happiness. This straightforward but effective method gauges consumer loyalty by asking them how likely they are to refer a good or service to others. By examining patterns over time, an analysis of NPS can provide insight into changes in customer sentiment. A decrease in the NPS can indicate areas that require improvement, while a high NPS typically indicates good value communication.

DEEPER INVESTIGATION of client experiences is made possible by using follow-up interviews. Direct client interaction generates meaningful dialogues that reveal experiences and feelings that are frequently left unsaid in surveys. These conversations provide an opportunity to ask open-ended enquiries, deep into what customers enjoy about a product and what may be improved. The qualitative feedback enhances the understanding of client perceptions by supplementing quantitative data.

Customer journey mapping is another technique to take into account. With the help of this graphic tool, the complete customer journey is laid out, with important touchpoints identified for satisfaction assessments. Plotting every interaction from the point of initial awareness to the follow-up after a purchase allows organisations to determine where consumers are appreciated and where they run into problems. This comprehensive approach enables focused enhancements that raise satisfaction levels everywhere.

Monitoring social media is a contemporary method of determining consumer mood. When consumers post about their experiences online, businesses may monitor mentions and levels of engagement across several channels. Examining likes, shares, and comments can be used to find trends in customer satisfaction. Positive criticism offers a chance for improvement, while constructive criticism can be acknowledged and welcomed.

INTERACTING WITH CLIENTS on social media creates a feeling of belonging and demonstrates that their opinions are valued.

Establishing loyalty programs also opens you a direct channel of connection with clients. These programs provide insights into the tastes and behaviours of their customers in addition to rewarding recurring business. Through the analysis of loyalty member involvement and feedback, companies can better customise their services to better meet the needs of their customers.

Deeper connection is cultivated as a result, increasing loyalty and general contentment.

Interactions with customer service offer yet another useful way to gauge satisfaction. Tracking metrics like response time, resolution rate, and customer feedback after support contacts helps illustrate how successfully value is provided during these important moments. Consumers are more likely to feel happy and appreciated when they receive prompt, useful responses, which will increase their brand loyalty.

Numerous insights about customer satisfaction can be gained by looking at retention rates. High retention rates are frequently a sign that consumers think their relationship with a brand will always be valuable. On the other hand, a high churn rate indicates discontent. Understanding the causes of churn can help with improvement by providing information about what has to be altered to better satisfy customers.

⟨⟨⟩⟩

PARTICIPATING IN FOCUS groups with consumers can also provide insightful information. Bringing together a varied set of clients offers a forum for candid conversations about their perceptions of the brand, expectations, and experiences. These meetings have the power to unearth nuggets of wisdom that let companies modify their plans in response to immediate input from their target market. This collaborative strategy promotes consumer relationships, generating a sense of involvement in shaping the brand.

Online reviews and ratings provide another way to gauge satisfaction. Consumers voluntarily post their thoughts on websites that are industry-specific or on platforms like Yelp and Google. An abundance of knowledge regarding consumer experiences can be obtained by keeping an eye on and evaluating this feedback. Negative reviews draw attention to areas that need improvement, while positive evaluations demonstrate valuable communication that is done well. Reactions to reviews, whether favourable or unfavourable, show that the business respects client feedback and is dedicated to development.

Customer satisfaction can be measured more effectively by making use of feedback loops. Through the implementation of systems for routinely collecting and evaluating client feedback, companies may adjust to evolving tastes and demands. By having a constant conversation with customers, businesses are able to build dynamic relationships that help them stay ahead of the curve and improve their value offers over time.

Adopting benchmarks for customer satisfaction also makes it easier to compare performance to industry norms. Contextualising a company's position vis-à-vis its rivals helps explain consumer satisfaction levels. Organisations might be motivated to innovate and improve their value communication methods by using this information to inform strategic decisions.

The Long-Term Impact of Value Communication

Examining the enduring consequences of proficient value communication unveils an abundance of advantages capable of revolutionising an enterprise. Imagine a market where businesses build rapport with clients to convert sporadic purchasers into devoted supporters. This transformation unfolds through many real-world examples and case studies that highlight how mastering the art of talking value leads to recurrent business and enthusiastic referrals.

Consider a well-known coffee chain that decided to sell experiences rather than just coffee. They developed a story around their products by highlighting the superiority of their beans, the skill of their baristas, and the welcoming ambiance of their locations. Customers responded well to this strategy, starting to perceive their coffee purchases as investments in community and quality. What was the outcome? a notable rise in recurring business. Frequent patrons typically shared their excitement with friends and family, coming for the full experience rather than simply the caffeine fix. Their devotion paid off in the form of solid sales results and a powerful brand presence.

Think about a software company that used a consultative approach with its clients in the technology sector. Rather than focussing on making quick sales, their sales team had in-depth discussions about the particular requirements and difficulties that prospective customers experienced. They gained trust by presenting their software as a customised solution as opposed to just a product.

This approach eventually produced a devoted following of clients who came to them for updates and new products. Content clients turned champions, recommending the business to others in their circles, and so on, all without incurring significant advertising costs.

A high-end skincare company provides yet another striking illustration. This company concentrated on teaching consumers about skin health and the science underlying their formulas rather than just selling items.

By means of workshops, webinars, and captivating social media material, they positioned themselves as reliable skincare advisers. Customers who felt empowered with knowledge were more inclined to return for subsequent purchases, looking to expand their routines with new products. Their dedication to communication created a feeling of community and a devoted following that frequently posted about their experiences online, increasing brand awareness through real-life recommendations.

The significance of human touches in the retail industry should not be overlooked. Remarkable outcomes were achieved by a small boutique that values connections with its customers more than just transactions. The proprietor took great care to recall each client's name, preferences, and even noteworthy events like birthdays. Their provision of customised suggestions and handwritten expressions of gratitude fostered a friendly and inviting atmosphere. Feeling respected and appreciated resulted in not only recurring business but also sincere recommendations to friends. Real connections, as opposed to conventional advertising, were what propelled the growth of word-of-mouth advertising.

Examining the service sector provides more illustrations of the advantages of value communication. A well-known restaurant business made an investment in educating employees to provide outstanding customer service while emphasising the calibre and origin of their food. Through stories about the dishes, servers connected patrons to nearby farmers and sustainable farming methods.

This strategy gave clients a sense of belonging to a greater story. What was the outcome? a devoted following that frequented the restaurant on a regular basis, attracted not only by the cuisine but also by the ideals it represented. They frequently extended invitations to friends to join, which led to a consistent stream of new customers through positive referrals.

Analysing the automobile sector identifies similar trends. The reputation of an auto dealership was significantly altered when it shifted its focus from aggressive sales tactics to open communication and customer education. The dealership positioned itself as a partner in the car-buying process by offering comprehensive information about automobiles, financing choices, and maintenance. Clients valued this candour, which resulted in enduring bonds and recurring business. With time, these contented clients evolved into brand evangelists, spreading the word about their great encounters and resulting in recommendations that accelerated the dealership's expansion.

It's the same thing in the realm of e-commerce. An online shop changed its business model by prioritising post-purchase engagement and customer assistance. Following a customer's purchase, the business sent them personalised emails with usage guidelines, maintenance instructions, and special offers for subsequent purchases. This tactic let one-time purchasers feel a connection to the brand and encouraged them to return. Positive customer reviews were common, which served as social proof to draw in new customers and emphasised the significance of excellent value communication.

The success stories in the field of value communication reveal a common thread: when organisations focus on the long-term benefits of customer relationships, the returns are enormous. Sincere interaction with customers fosters loyalty since they are more inclined to return and refer others to the company. Value communication has a transforming effect that goes beyond quick sales to create a long-lasting company strategy based on client loyalty and trust.

In this procedure, comprehending client input is also very important. Businesses that actively seek out and respond to criticism show that they are dedicated to making improvements. By implementing improvements based on client feedback, businesses not only better their offerings but also build a culture of collaboration. Client loyalty is fuelled by their sense of engagement and being heard. Customers that are happy are frequently happy to tell others about their good experiences, which starts a positive feedback loop that drives business expansion.

SUMMARY

Gaining proficiency in value discussions changes the way companies interact with their clients. Envision entering a world where value is mostly irrelevant and the experiences, gains, and connections made along the journey are what count most. It's about shifting perceptions, developing interactions that connect, and weaving value into every interaction.

Think back to your first interactions with possible clients.

CONSIDER THE VALUE of storytelling rather than jumping to the presentation of figures. Providing engaging stories about how a good or service has improved people's lives sparks curiosity. These narratives create connections and arouse feelings that numbers cannot. Using relatable experiences to engage prospective customers not only draws them in but also establishes the groundwork for deep connections.

IT'S CRITICAL TO REFOCUS attention on the value offered when responding to frequent concerns about pricing. A client might raise concerns about the price of a high-end product, for instance. You can change their mind by responding with a story that emphasises the investment's long-term savings, durability, and special features. Consumers start to see value and benefits more broadly and look past the initial cost. This strategy fosters trust and improves the clientele's experience in general.

EFFECTIVE VALUE COMMUNICATION training for staff members is crucial to this change. Employees who are given the resources to meaningfully interact with consumers become brand ambassadors. Team members develop active listening and intelligent response through role-playing exercises and real-world scenarios. They welcome the notion that each encounter with a consumer offers the chance to establish rapport and leave a lasting impression.

THIS SHIFT IN CULTURE promotes an atmosphere where connections are valued more highly than transactions.

Client feedback provides insightful information about how effectively a company conveys value. Asking for feedback and ideas on a regular basis empowers clients and shows that you are dedicated to making improvements. This feedback loop allows firms to adjust their offers and increases the client experience. Businesses that incorporate consumer input into their product development and service innovations not only meet but surpass customer expectations, but also cultivate devoted advocates who enthusiastically share their experiences.

Assessing client happiness offers a tangible method for evaluating value communication efficacy. Following up with surveys and feedback forms helps businesses find out what people think and where they can make improvements. By analysing this data, trends can be identified, such as the features of the good or service that appeal to customers the most.

This knowledge informs choices and propels the business model's ongoing development, guaranteeing that value is at the centre of every plan.

Long-term impacts manifest through the building of client loyalty. Continuing to interact with clients after the transaction promotes referrals and repeat business. Businesses stay at the forefront of their customers' minds by staying in constant communication, whether it is through newsletters, tailored follow-ups, or unique deals.

Customers love being remembered and respected, which transforms them into enthusiastic advocates. This natural expansion increases the brand's reach and influence by creating a positive feedback loop with happy customers bringing in new ones.

Establishing a customer-focused culture in an organisation is essential to its success. Value communication is not just the sales team's job; employees at all levels should accept this approach. From product development to customer service to marketing, every area contributes to providing value. By ensuring that clients receive a consistent message and experience, this all-encompassing strategy reinforces the idea that their satisfaction is the ultimate goal.

Numerous industries provide examples of how excellent value communication can transform an organisation. When a retailer engages in customer education regarding sustainable practices, it not only improves the shopping experience but also cultivates brand loyalty among consumers who care about the environment.

Consumers who identify with a cause develop strong brand advocates and frequently post about their experiences on social media.

Within the technology industry, organisations that offer comprehensive onboarding procedures to new employees foster a feeling of acceptance and assurance. These companies show their dedication to the success of their clients by providing training and continuing assistance. Users that feel empowered are more inclined to explore advanced features and suggest the product to others, encouraging organic growth.

The significance of value communication is evident even in the service sector, where connections are crucial. Loyalty is fostered by a spa that values its ties with clients by providing customised experiences and follow-up consultations. A community of advocates is created when customers feel appreciated and are more likely to use the service again and refer others to it.

Businesses engaged in e-commerce can also profit from prioritising value over price.

These brands deliver a rich buying experience through interactive content, user-generated reviews, and extensive product descriptions. Consumers are more satisfied and likely to make more purchases when they feel knowledgeable and confident about their choices.

Navigating value communication requires a thorough understanding of the competitive landscape. Companies have to keep up with consumer preferences and market developments to make sure their products and services meet the expectations of their clients. Companies are able to maintain their relevance and responsiveness because to this adaptability, which strengthens their standing as industry leaders.

Authenticity is the lifeblood of value communication. When a brand is sincere in its attempts to deliver value, customers can tell. Establishing trust-based relationships calls for openness, truthfulness, and consistency.

Businesses that follow these guidelines encourage a sense of loyalty that goes beyond sales and turns clients into devoted supporters.

STRATEGIC ACTION PLAN FOR MASTERING VALUE COMMUNICATION

O bjective
Enhance customer relationships by focusing on value communication, leading to increased customer satisfaction, loyalty, and long-term business growth.

1. Assess Current Communication Practices

- **Action Steps:**

- Conduct an internal audit of current sales and communication techniques.

- Gather feedback from team members about common challenges in discussing price versus value.

- Identify key areas where value communication can be improved.

- **Timeline: 2 weeks**

- **Responsible Parties:** Sales Manager, Team Leads

2. Develop Value-Focused Training Program

- **Action Steps:**

- Design a training curriculum that emphasizes storytelling, customer engagement, and the benefits of products/services.

- Include role-playing scenarios to practice handling price objections.

- Schedule regular training sessions to keep the team updated on best practices.

- **Timeline:** 1 month for development; ongoing sessions every quarter

- **Responsible Parties:** Human Resources, Training Coordinator

3. IMPLEMENT CUSTOMER Feedback Mechanisms

- **Action Steps:**

- Create surveys and feedback forms post-purchase to assess customer perceptions of value.

- Analyze feedback to identify trends and areas for improvement.

- Share insights with the team to inform ongoing strategy adjustments.

- **Timeline:** Start within 1 month and continuously collect data

- **Responsible Parties:** Customer Service Team, Marketing Team

4. Foster a Customer-Centric Culture

- **Action Steps:**

- Promote the importance of customer relationships at all levels of the organization.

- Encourage all departments to contribute to value creation (e.g., marketing should emphasize benefits, not just features).

- Recognize and reward employees who exemplify value communication in their roles.

- **Timeline:** Ongoing

- **Responsible Parties:** Executive Leadership, Department Heads

5. CREATE COMPELLING Customer Stories

- **Action Steps:**

- Collect and curate customer success stories that highlight the benefits and value of products/services.

- Share these stories through various channels (website, social media, newsletters) to illustrate real-world impact.

- Encourage satisfied customers to become brand advocates by sharing their experiences publicly.

- **Timeline:** 2 months for initial collection; ongoing updates

- **Responsible Parties:** Marketing Team, Content Creators

6. MEASURE SUCCESS and Adjust Strategy

- **Action Steps:**

- Establish key performance indicators (KPIs) to measure the effectiveness of value communication (e.g., customer satisfaction scores, repeat purchase rates).

- Review results quarterly and adjust strategies based on data and feedback.
- Share results with the entire team to highlight successes and areas for improvement.
  - **Timeline:** Quarterly reviews
  - **Responsible Parties:** Management Team, Data Analyst

7. ENGAGE CUSTOMERS Beyond Transactions
  - **Action Steps:**
  - Develop loyalty programs that reward customers for repeat business.
  - Create engaging content that provides value (e.g., tips, educational resources) beyond product promotions.
  - Host events or webinars that foster community and encourage customer interaction.
  - **Timeline:** Initial program launch within 3 months; ongoing engagement
  - **Responsible Parties:** Marketing Team, Community Managers

8. LEVERAGE TECHNOLOGY for Better Engagement
  - **Action Steps:**
  - Utilize CRM tools to track customer interactions and preferences, enabling personalized communication.
  - Implement chatbots or AI-driven solutions for immediate customer support, enhancing the value proposition.
  - Regularly update digital platforms to ensure they communicate value effectively.
  - **Timeline:** 2-3 months for implementation; continuous improvement
  - **Responsible Parties:** IT Department, Customer Service Team

CONCLUSION
This action plan provides a roadmap for readers to elevate their approach to customer interactions by prioritizing value communication. By taking these

steps, businesses can strengthen relationships, foster loyalty, and achieve sustainable growth. Encourage readers to adapt the plan according to their unique business contexts and continuously seek ways to enhance the value they deliver to customers.

Don't miss out!

Visit the website below and you can sign up to receive emails whenever JOSHUA ZAGHE publishes a new book. There's no charge and no obligation.

https://books2read.com/r/B-A-BINQB-JEPBF

BOOKS 2 READ

Connecting independent readers to independent writers.

Did you love *Never Talk Price to a Customer: How to Master the Art of Talking Value*? Then you should read *How to Turn Attention into Customers : Mastering the Art of Transforming Attention into Loyal Customers*[1] by JOSHUA ZAGHE!

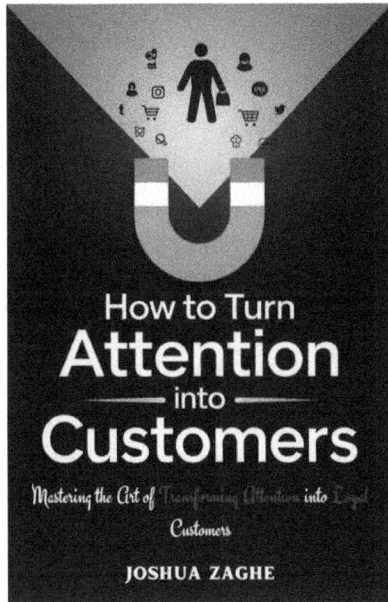

Imagine capturing attention in a world bursting with noise, where every second your customers are pulled in a thousand directions. The art of turning a fleeting glance into lasting engagement isn't some mystical formula but a crafted skill. It's about grabbing that elusive moment when eyes lock, curiosity sparks, and suddenly, they can't look away. This isn't just about being seen—it's about captivating. Forget the generic fluff that floods the market; this book brings you strategies that pierce through the chaos, making you not just visible but unforgettable. Dive into real-world tactics that turn mere interest into deep-seated loyalty, compelling your audience to not just notice but to crave what you offer.

Your audience's interest doesn't stop at just knowing you exist—they need a reason to care, and that's where it gets exciting. It's about connecting on a

---

1. https://books2read.com/u/mg6R87

2. https://books2read.com/u/mg6R87

level that goes beyond products or services. Why do some brands make us feel something, while others fade into the background? The secret lies in creating an emotional bond, weaving stories that resonate so deeply that customers don't just purchase—they believe. This is about tapping into desires and solving problems they didn't even know they had. Through captivating narratives, personalized experiences, and authentic interactions, you'll learn how to spark that 'aha' moment. It's about crafting messages that make them lean in, their curiosity growing with every word, every image, every touchpoint. Turn passive onlookers into active participants, keeping them hooked and eager for more.

It's not enough to capture interest—you have to fan those flames into a burning desire. This book is your guide to building a magnetic presence that pulls customers closer, making them feel like they're part of something bigger. Picture this: customers are not just reaching for their wallets; they're reaching for an experience, a solution that speaks directly to their needs. Every brand wants loyalty, but this is about creating an irresistible pull that keeps them coming back, not because they have to, but because they want to. Through unique positioning, value-packed offers, and creating a sense of exclusivity, you'll learn how to make your brand not just an option but *the* choice. Imagine your customers feeling that twinge of excitement at every new release, every update, eager to share their experience, becoming advocates without even realizing it. This is about transforming that casual interest into a powerful, almost magnetic force that turns customers into lifelong fans.

And now, the final step—turning desire into action. This book doesn't leave you hanging with just theories and ideas; it arms you with actionable strategies that make it easy for your customers to say, "Yes, I'm in!" We're talking about creating frictionless journeys where every click, every interaction, moves them seamlessly closer to hitting that buy button. Learn to craft calls-to-action that aren't pushy but persuasive, making it a no-brainer for them to choose you. It's about setting the stage where the next step feels natural, almost inevitable. From mastering the art of persuasion to leveraging psychological triggers, you'll gain insights that turn curiosity into commitment, and interest into investment. And the best part? These strategies aren't just about getting that first sale—they're about creating cycles of engagement that keep customers coming back, again and again.

No more shouting into the void, hoping for attention. It's time to make waves. Grab this book and start transforming the way you attract, engage, and retain customers, creating a loyal following that doesn't just buy—they advocate, they share, they grow with you. This is your blueprint to not just survive in the crowded market but to thrive, turning every interaction into an opportunity for lasting connection and unstoppable growth.

Also by JOSHUA ZAGHE

9 798227 621962